Exploring Leadership

Facilitation and Activity Guide

The Jossey-Bass

Higher and Adult Education Series

Exploring
Leadership

⌄

For College Students Who Want to **Make a Difference**

Facilitation and Activity Guide

Wendy **Wagner**
Daniel T. **Ostick**
and **Associates**

JOSSEY-BASS
A Wiley Imprint
www.josseybass.com

CONTENTS

ABOUT THE AUTHORS

Wendy Wagner is an assistant professor of leadership and community engagement in New Century College at George Mason University. She is also the director of the Center for Leadership and Community Engagement and coordinator of the Leadership and Community Engagement Living Learning Community. Wendy's scholarship is related to civic engagement, leadership development for social change, and the scholarship of teaching and learning. In 2010 she received the Association of American Colleges and Universities' K. Patricia Cross Award recognizing future leaders of higher education in the areas of civic responsibility, teaching, and learning. At George Mason University, Wendy teaches courses on leadership, community based research, and community engagement. She was coeditor of *Leadership for a Better World* (2009) and the *Handbook for Student Leadership Development Programs* (2010). Wendy earned her PhD in College Student Personnel from the University of Maryland, her master's in College Student Personnel from Bowling Green State University, and her undergraduate degree in Communication Studies from the University of Nebraska–Lincoln.

Daniel T. Ostick serves as the coordinator for leadership curriculum development and academic partnerships in the Adele H. Stamp Student Union–Center for Campus Life at the University of Maryland. Daniel regularly teaches coursework on leadership theory and global leadership, and has published articles and chapters on the Social Change Model of Leadership, diversity and leadership, and LGBT issues and leadership. Prior to his current position, he held positions in residence life at the University of Maryland, the University of Texas at Austin, and the University of Illinois at Urbana-Champaign. Daniel earned his PhD in College Student Personnel from the University of Maryland, received his master's in College Student Personnel Administration from Indiana University, and obtained his undergraduate degree in advertising from the University of Georgia.

INTRODUCTION

Exploring Leadership (3rd edition) defines leadership as, "a relational and ethical process of people together attempting to accomplish positive change." When leadership is approached in this way, working with others to accomplish change, everyone can be a leader. Starting with that assumption creates our opportunity as leadership educators to help students explore their own strengths, experiences, and style in order to engage with others in a way that feels authentic and true to them. *Exploring Leadership* addresses these issues through the following sections:

Leadership for a Changing World. Understanding leadership—an overview of how leadership has been perceived differently over the years, why modern realities call for new approaches to leadership, and the presentation of the authors' relational leadership model.

Exploring Your Potential for Leadership. Understanding yourself and others—an exploration of students' own strengths, values, and ways of being in relation to others, as well as a discussion of the importance of ethics, character, and integrity.

Context for the Practice of Leadership. Understanding groups and organizations—a discussion of group development, group processes, and the complexity of leadership in organizations that comprise many intersecting groups.

Making a Difference with Leadership. Understanding the nature of change and thriving together—an exploration of the processes of change and how change is influenced and how leaders can work together in ways that utilize strengths and promote well-being for all in order to have the persistence and resilience that leadership requires.

> This Guide

The purpose of the *Facilitation and Activity Guide* is to provide active learning strategies for organizing a course or workshop series around *Exploring Leadership* (3rd edition). Each chapter in *Exploring Leadership* is addressed here through a set of one-hour Active Learning Modules. The Active Learning Modules are identified by a number and letter, with the number corresponding to the chapter of *Exploring Leadership* it supports. In addition, each chapter has a corresponding unit in the *Exploring Leadership: Student Workbook*.

The Active Learning Modules have been designed by some of the best leadership educators in higher education today, based on their particular areas of expertise and the classroom exercises they have personally found to be effective with their students. We have thoroughly enjoyed learning from them.

The Active Learning Modules are effective in either curricular or co-curricular settings and can be structured to build on each other or stand alone, depending on your purposes. The *Exploring Leadership: Student Workbook*, which provides worksheets and discussion questions that align with many of these modules, is a useful companion to this publication for either setting.

We hope you enjoy exploring new ways to actively engage your students with *Exploring Leadership*.

Wendy Wagner, George Mason University
Daniel Ostick, University of Maryland, College Park

Teaching Leadership | Wendy Wagner

> The Challenges of Leadership Education

As much as we enjoy our work, teaching leadership presents unique challenges. Leadership is a concept that is elusive. There are no clear-cut rules or formulas. Depending on their developmental readiness, many students come to us expecting clearly defined steps to leadership excellence. They can become frustrated by our efforts to help them learn to navigate ambiguity, recognize the influence of context, and have more complex consideration of relationships, organizations, and the process of influencing change.

There is an emotional as well as intellectual aspect of teaching leadership. We give students different lenses through which they consider their actions, including their previous approaches. It is a difficult thing to feel disappointed by or even ashamed of one's own prior behavior. Learning from those experiences cannot happen before those difficult emotions are attended to.

Complicating matters further, students do not come to leadership as blank slates. They have assumptions about leadership that are based on popular culture rather than social science. Their life experiences have also informed their beliefs about leadership, and those need to be honored, even as we sometimes challenge their interpretation of those events. Finally, our students practice leadership in a wide variety of contexts and need space to explore how approaches that work for others in some settings may or may not work for them in theirs.

› Attending to Knowing, Being, and Doing

Teaching leadership is also complicated because it is a topic for which the understanding of concepts and ability to apply them in context are distinct learning objectives. Many leadership educators find that teaching for the former in no way guarantees the latter.

While it is important for students to know key theories and models, true understanding involves being able to apply that knowledge and make meaning out of experiences in more informed ways. It is not what terms or theories students can accurately describe that counts, but whether their learning has transformed how they act. There are few fields in which the ability to take theory into practice is more important than in leadership. *Exploring Leadership* addresses this need through the model of "knowing, being, and doing" (Chapter 3). It requires that leadership classrooms address leadership content in terms of

- *Knowing.* Understanding from an intellectual standpoint. Learning new theories and models and being able to analyze situations through them.
- *Being.* Understanding the implications of the content from a personal standpoint. Learning to be the person the world needs leaders to be. Students wrestle with how to *be* ethical, open, inclusive, process-oriented, and so forth.
- *Doing.* Being capable of acting in ways that align with this content. Having interpersonal skills, the ability to self-monitor.

› Attending to Self-efficacy

Leadership self-efficacy refers the extent to which a person believes they are capable of being an effective leader. Efficacy is distinct from capacity. Whether students believe they can and whether they actually can are separate issues, and yet recent research is revealing that developing the capacity to do leadership and having self-efficacy for it are intertwined (Dugan & Komives, 2010). People generally avoid tasks they think they cannot do and situations they do not believe they can handle. Since significant learning happens from experience, students with low self-efficacy are therefore limiting the learning experiences they will have.

So how do leadership educators address self-efficacy in order to affect the building of capacity? Bandura's work on self-efficacy (1997) described four sources of enhancing an individual's internal belief system and informs the ways that leadership educators can address this issue:

- *Mastery experiences.* Direct experiences that enhance skills that can be generalized to other contexts.
- *Vicarious experiences.* Observations of others (particularly peers) successfully performing challenging leadership tasks and roles.
- *Verbal persuasion.* Encouragement from advisors and peers that the student is capable.
- *Assessment of physiological and affective states.* Learning reflective and mindfulness techniques to recognize signs of stress and anxiety and respond proactively.

> Effective Teaching

A discussion of effective teaching strategies for any discipline are worth reviewing as we consider our effectiveness as leadership educators. A study of excellent professors representing a variety of fields (Bain, 2004) identified several key concepts that are worth our consideration.

- *They believe knowledge is constructed rather than received.* Excellent teachers think of their work as "stimulating construction, not transmitting knowledge" (p. 27).

- *They recognize that mental models change slowly.* Concepts that require complexity of thought are often counterintuitive to the models students have constructed based on everyday experience. Building new models requires that (1) students face a scenario in which their current mental model will not work, (2) they care enough about it to wrestle with it, and (3) they handle the emotions that result when long-held beliefs no longer work.
- *They believe questions are crucial.* Questions point out holes in our mental models. Getting students to develop their own questions is fundamental to their transition to using new a new mental model and to their capacity for lifelong learning.
- *They know that getting students to care is the key.* When we convince students to care about their own leadership development, our work is half done.

Perhaps the best advice resulting from Bain's study is this, "Start with the students rather than the discipline" (2004). To understand students' existing mental models and know what questions will capture their attention and inspire them to care about learning leadership, we need to start with knowing who students are, what they care about, and what they already know. We need to understand the contexts in which they practice leadership. We need to understand the ways that culture, gender, family, popular media, and the shared historic experiences of a generation have shaped their mental models. By starting with what students know and how they know it, we invite them to have an opinion about the course material from the beginning and therefore to have a role in their own learning.

> Active Learning

It is the assumption of the *Facilitation and Activity Guide* that active learning environments are the most effective way to foster leadership learning. Students in an active learning community do not simply listen as information is "transmitted." Instead, they are involved in Bloom's (1956) higher levels of thinking: application, analysis, synthesis, and, ultimately, in evaluating the topic on their own terms.

As leadership educators, we think of ourselves as facilitators of a learning process rather than as conveyors of wisdom. We create a learning environment, shape a structure for students to engage in, monitor their experience with it, and guide them to reach their own conclusions. Thomas Wren described teaching leadership as whitewater teaching, "Things move along rapidly, often in unpredictable channels, and the identical exercise rarely plays out the same way twice. However, the issues likely to arise are predictable in a general sense" (Wren, 2001, p. 6). The learning modules in this guide are aimed at helping instructors navigate that whitewater.

> Facilitating the Experience

As the facilitator of active learning, there are several important issues to consider.

Creating Community

"Students will engage more in classroom-based learning if they feel that they are welcomed, valuable, contributing members of a learning community" (Barkley, 2010, p. 110). In order to foster that kind of community, educators must address several issues:

Attention to the physical space. The setting needs to be as comfortable as possible and designed to foster active participation. For example, students might be seated in one large discussion circle, in pods of small groups, or they may spend the better part of some learning modules not seated at all.

Attention to interpersonal interactions and civility. This involves allowing time for students to get to know each other and setting expectations and norms related to participating and including others in discussions.

Attention to creating an inclusive environment. Using examples and contexts that are representative in terms of cultural communities, gender, sexual orientation, social class, and traditional or nontraditionally aged students.

Developing Habits for Experiential Learning

As engaging as the activities in these Active Learning Modules are, the experiential learning literature is clear that learning occurs not just from activities but from a cycle of experience, reflection, generalization and application (Kolb, 1981). Each Active Learning Module includes useful questions for guiding students in this process.

Aligning Structure with Developmental Readiness

Students vary in the extent of their cognitive development and the learning environment should be designed to be optimal for students' readiness. Structure—the amount of framework and direction provided to students—is a critical element for designing learning environments. The level of ambiguity in the learning environment should be appropriate for students' level of cognitive development (Miller, Groccia, & Wilkes, 1996).

Early stages of development   Students in early stages of cognitive development operate from the assumption that there is one "right" answer to any given question. They expect people in authority (i.e., the facilitator) to have that answer and share it (Perry, 1981). These students benefit from having clear frameworks and a lot of direction about how to approach each activity. They need to be directly guided through the reflection process by having steps outlined for them and a set of questions they are to address.

Later stages of development   Students in later stages of cognitive development are able to benefit from the perspectives of other participants, as well as the facilitator's, on the given topic. They are also better equipped to deal with ambiguity and guide their own learning (Perry, 1981). These students do better with a looser structure, one that allows them to come up with their own way to approach an experience and the ensuing reflective discussion. They may come up with their own reflection questions for each other, rather than expecting the facilitator to fully guide that process. They appreciate being given room to more deeply explore the aspects of the topic that interest them, rather than having to stick closely to a facilitator's preplanned questions.

Monitoring Participants and Oneself

It is a reality in active learning environments that the same activity rarely plays out the same way twice. Unique personalities mean students will interact with each other in different ways. Unique personal histories mean students will find personal connections to the topic in different ways. You may be providing the same river, but each group of students will navigate the bends in it their own way. Monitoring that navigation is an important facilitator role.

Attention to participants. Pay attention to nonverbal cues, the energy in the room, whether some participants are dominating the conversation and others are being interrupted. Give quiet participants room to share. Don't assume that silence means agreement or disinterest.

Attention to oneself. How much are you talking compared to participants? Who are you calling on? What messages are your own nonverbal communications sending? Where you are situated in relation to participants, and does that position communicate what you intend it to?

> References

Bain, K. (2004). *What the best college teachers do*. Cambridge, MA: Harvard University Press.

Bandura, A. (1997). *Self-efficacy: The exercise of control*. New York: Freeman.

Barkley, E. F. (2010). *Student engagement techniques: A handbook for college faculty*. San Francisco: Jossey-Bass.

Bloom, B. S. (Ed.) (1956). *Taxonomy of educational objectives*. Boston, MA: Allyn and Bacon.

Dugan, J. P., & Komives, S. R. (2010). Influences on college students' capacity for socially responsible leadership. *Journal of College Student Development*, **51**, 525–549.

Kolb, D. A. (1981). Learning styles and disciplinary differences. In A. W. Chickering & Associates (Eds.), *The modern American college: Responding to the new realities of diverse students and a changing society* (pp. 232–255). San Francisco: Jossey-Bass.

Miller, J. E., Groccia, J. E., & Wilkes, J. M. (1996). Providing structure: The critical element. In *New Directions for Teaching and Learning No. 67*. San Francisco: Jossey-Bass.

Perry, W. G. (1981). Cognitive and ethical growth: The making of meaning. In A. W. Chickering & Associates (Eds.), *The modern American college* (pp. 76–116). San Francisco: Jossey-bassBass.

Wren, J. T. (2001). *Instructor's manual to accompany The Leader's Companion*. Richmond, VA: Jepson School of Leadership Studies, University of Richmond.

Leadership Identity Development

Wendy Wagner

As was described in the last chapter, leadership educators attend to much more than simply the cognitive understanding of leadership theory. Leadership development also involves building capacity to do leadership and addressing student self-efficacy to engage with others and have an influence for change. Leadership development also requires that we address issues related to identity, that is, how students see themselves.

Erikson (1968) described identity as a sense of a continuous self that is discovered through interaction with others in a variety of social contexts. We help students become conscious of aspects of their identity through a continual cycle of observation and reflection. Identity development models involve a process in which students (1) become aware of certain aspects of themselves that are different from others around them (differentiation) and (2) weave that aspect into their sense of themselves as a whole (integration) (Pascarella & Terenzini, 2005).

Identity formation includes integration of many aspects of identity that are related to our social groups. Students "take on the norms and expectation of a role such as an athlete identity, a fraternity identity, a graduate student identity, an air force officer identity, or a lawyer identity. Being a leader can also be a social identity" (Komives, Lucas, & McMahon, 2007, p. 392). Some identity groups, such as gender, sexual orientation, race or ethnic identity, involve students not only making meaning of a sense of self, but also understanding power and privilege issues that come with those identities. Many times it is a new awareness of privilege issues that makes these identities particularly salient aspects of the self during college.

In some cases, it is the intersection of identities that can cause inner struggle. For example, establishing a healthy sense of self as a gay man within certain ethnic or religious groups that are not accepting of homosexuality is a complex undertaking that benefits from a caring support network (Komives et al., 2007). These social identities also intersect with one's sense of leader identity. Societal expectations of "normal" gendered behavior, for example, affect the ways men and women approach their leader roles differently.

> Leadership Identity Development

Researchers on how a relational leadership identity develops over time have created a stage model that helps us understand how students see themselves during several points along this journey (Komives et al., 2005). The journey to the relational approach to leadership that *Exploring Leadership* espouses is a gradual process described by the stages in this model.

Leadership Identity Development Stages

LID Stages	Stage Description	Sample Identity Statement
(1) Awareness	Becoming aware of how some people lead and influence others. Usually an external other person, like the U.S. president or a historic figure like Martin Luther King Jr. [feels dependent on others]	A leader is someone out there, not me.
(2) Exploration/ Engagement	Immersion in a breadth of group experiences (e.g., Scouts, youth group, swim team) to make friends and find a fit. [feels dependent on others]	Maybe I could be a leader.

LID Stages	Stage Description	Sample Identity Statement
(3) Leader Identified	Fully involved in organizations and groups. Holds a belief that the positional leader does leadership whereas others do followership. [may be independent from others (being a leader), dependent on others (being a follower), or hold both views]	If I am the leader, it is my responsibility to get the job done. If I am a follower, I need to help the leader get the job done.
(4) Leadership Differentiated	Recognizes that leadership comes from all around in an organization; as a positional leader, seeks to be a facilitator and practices shared leadership; as a member, knows one is engaged in doing leadership. [feels interdependent with others]	I can be a leader even if I am not the leader and I see that leadership is also a process. We do leadership together.
(5) Generativity	Is concerned about the sustainability of the group and seeks to develop others; is concerned about personal passion to leave a legacy and have one's actions make a difference. [feels interdependent with others]	We all need to develop leadership in the organization and in others. I am responsible to serve the organization.
(6) Integration/Synthesis	Leadership capacity is an internalized part of oneself and part of the perspective one brings to all situations. [feels interdependent with others]	I can work with others to accomplish shared goals and work for change.

Source: Adapted from Komives, Longerbeam, Owen, Mainella, & Osteen (2006).

Generally, students are in stage three when they arrive at college. They have participated in organizations already in high school clubs, church groups, and in part-time jobs. These students have a hierarchical view of organizations and leader roles, with some wanting the leader role (the "independent" view of stage three) and others avoiding them (the "dependent" view).

As leadership educators, we are particularly interested in what this study identified as the key influences on leadership identity development. The key categories were developing the self, group influences, changing view of self with others, broadening view of leadership, and certain developmental influences.

Key Categories		Implications for Educators
Developing the Self	Students experience increasing levels of self-awareness, self-confidence, interpersonal and other leadership skills, and expanded motivations (from joining groups to make friends to being involved in order to contribute to changes they believe in).	Provide opportunities to be reflective about issues related to self-awareness and sense of life purpose. Encourage students to take on new roles in order to build new skills. Provide stage-appropriate skill-building opportunities. For example, learning to delegate in stage three lays a foundation for having the trust to work collaboratively in stage four.
Group Influences	Meaningful engagement in groups results in more complex understanding of them. Deeper awareness of the influence of organization structure and of groups as part of a larger system that could build coalitions for larger change. Continuity of membership in a group is key to this development.	Encourage students to stay with at least one key group. Promote deep involvement in one or two groups rather than shallow engagement in many groups.

Key Categories		Implications for Educators
Changing View of Self with Others	Shifting perceptions of dependency on others. Begins by seeing self as dependent on others. Shifts to feelings of independence. Ends with realization that people are both dependent on others and depended upon by others: interdependence.	Encourage gradual shifts of awareness. Don't expect students in early stages to understand concepts that rely on the assumption of interdependence. Guide intentional reflection about being depended on as well as dependent upon.
Broadening View of Leadership	Shifting definition of what leadership is. Initially views leadership as something others do (political leaders, teachers or older peers). In time, has a positional leadership view, the person with the "title" (president, committee chair) is the leader. Ends by defining leadership as a relational process that all active participants are engaged in.	Recognize and support any student who makes contributions to the group. This helps all group members see that work as "doing leadership."
Developmental Influences	Supportive mentors, including both adults and peers, play an important role in development. Having meaningful involvement and reflection on learning from those experiences is also critical.	Prepare advisors and older students for mentorship roles. They should both encourage students to take on new experiences and serve as a sounding board for reflective meaning-making.

> Addressing Both Attitude and Behavior

It is noteworthy that some students in the study described leadership in relational terms, "My approach is to collaborate rather than dictate," but still behaved in groups in ways that emphasized leader/follower differentiation and hierarchical organization structures. At the same time, others students behaved in ways that were consistent with advanced relational stages, but did not have the language to describe themselves in that way, "I'm not a leader, it's just important to me that we get all of these people working together to make a difference on this issue."

The researchers concluded that this disconnect signals a transition between stages (Komives et al., 2005). The transition from one stage to the next may begin with behavior and the language follows, or it may begin with a change in attitude and the behavior follows. As Komives, Lucas, and McMahon (2007) described, "Some people need to think differently about something before they can act differently; others start acting differently and then stop to think about why" (p. 400). Our role as educators is to recognize that the student is experiencing some shift, be aware that he or she is likely feeling some dissonance, and serve as a supportive sounding board for their meaning-making and reflection.

Leadership educators interested in learning more about the leadership identity development model are encouraged to explore the following resources:

Komives, S. R., Longerbeam, S. D., Owen, J. E., Mainella, F. C., & Osteen, L. (2006). A leadership identity development model: Applications from a grounded theory. *Journal of College Student Development, 47*(4), 401–418.

Komives, S. R., Owen, J. E., Longerbeam, S. D., Mainella, F. C., & Osteen, L. (2005). Developing a leadership identity: A grounded theory. *Journal of College Student Development, 46*(6), 593–611.

Komives, S. R., Longerbeam, S. D., Mainella, F. C., Osteen, L., Owen, J. E., & Wagner W. (2009). Leadership identity development: Challenges in applying a developmental model. *Journal of Leadership Education, 8*(1), 11–47.

Wagner, W. (2011). Considerations of student development in leadership. In S. R. Komives, J. P. Dugan, J. E. Owen, C. Slack, & Wagner, W. (Eds.), *The handbook for student leadership development* (2nd ed). A publication of the National Clearinghouse for Leadership Programs. San Francisco, CA: Jossey-Bass.

A review of the development of a relational leadership identity is an important reminder of the ongoing nature of this process. When we provide students a good foundation of research-based leadership theory and the habit of combining experience with reflection, we are providing the tools for life-long learning about leadership.

> References

Erikson, E. H. (1968). *Identity: Youth and crisis.* New York: Norton.

Komives, S. R., Lucas, N., & McMahon, T. R. (2007). *Exploring Leadership: For College Students Who Want to Make a Difference* (2nd ed). San Francisco: Jossey-Bass.

Komives, S. R., Owen, J. E., Longerbeam, S. D., Mainella, F. C., & Osteen, L. (2005). Developing a leadership identity: A grounded theory. *Journal of College Student Development, 46,* 593–611.

Pascarella, E., & Terenzini, P. (2005). *How college affects students: A third decade of research* (Vol. 2). San Francisco: Jossey-Bass.

Active Learning Module 1a

Introduction to Leadership

Laura Osteen

> ## Summary of Concepts

This learning module addresses Chapter 1, An Introduction to Leadership. This chapter introduces students to leadership as a process of engaging with others in accomplishing change. It is within this relational, ethical leadership process that everyone can be a leader. Through engaging in a critical thinking process, each of us can come to understand our personal experiences, strengths, and values that guide our actions as we work with others toward change.

Six foundational principles of this emerging leadership paradigm are

1. Leadership is a concern of all of us.
2. Leadership is viewed and valued differently by various disciplines and cultures.
3. Conventional views of leadership have changed.
4. Leadership can be exhibited in many ways.
5. Leadership qualities and skills can be learned and developed.
6. Leadership committed to ethical action is needed to encourage change and social responsibility.

The chapter concludes with a discussion about the purposes of leadership and the need for student to be self-directed as leadership learners.

> Learning Outcomes

Students will

- Define their currently held beliefs on the behaviors of leadership and the characteristics of a leader
- Reflect on what they would like to know more about in the leadership process and the role of a leader
- Develop a leadership learning plan

> Module Overview

The module begins with a standing continuum activity in which students express their degree of agreement with a variety of leadership statements. Then students identify leaders and leadership behaviors, sharing their reflections in pairs. Finally, students individually reflect on a series of prompts related to their purposes for engaging in leadership and develop a plan to facilitate their own leadership learning.

Estimated Time
Activity 1: Leadership Paradigms Standing Continuum,
    15 minutes
Activity 2: Leaders and Leadership Behaviors Pair and Share,
    25 minutes
Activity 3: Responding to Reflection Prompts, 25 minutes

Materials/Supplies
Paper
Writing utensils

> Module Activities

Activity 1: Leadership Paradigms Standing Continuum

Time: 15 minutes

Goal: to gather reactions to the emergent paradigm of leadership and initiate interest in the critical importance of the foundational principles.

Introduction: The first chapter outlines beliefs about leaders and leadership. Let's start by reacting to and sharing our beliefs concerning these broad statements about leaders and leadership. These statements reflect different paradigms addressed in Chapter 1.

Create a continuum from *strongly agree* to *strongly disagree* in the room; you may use four corners of the room, or a single line, or if space is tight simply have students stand up if they agree.

Move or stand in place to show agreement or disagreement with each statement. Take a moment to see where you are standing in relation to your peers. If time allows, generate discussion by asking students why they chose to stand where they are standing.

- Leaders are born and not made.
- I can be a leader without a formal title or position within an organization.
- Leaders always work for good.
- Leadership is a process of creating change.
- Not everyone can be a leader.
- Who I am determines how I lead.
- If I can do it by myself it is not leadership.
- A central component of leadership is ethics.
- I am a leader.
- . . . Add statements that stand out for you from the chapter.

After going through each statement, share reactions in a large group and bridge to an overview of the foundational principles covered in Chapter 1. Debrief with the first reflection question found at the end of Chapter 1, "Which of the six foundational principles used to develop this book do you most closely agree with and why? Which is most difficult to endorse and why? Which is the most difficult to practice and why? Which is the easiest to practice and why?"

Activity 2: Leaders and Leadership Behaviors Pair and Share

Time: 25 minutes

Goal: to recognize the power of paradigms in excluding people from the language and practice of leaders. When we start from the paradigm of leadership as a position, we immediately exclude nonpositional leaders from the conversation.

Ask the following questions, one question at a time, allowing time to respond to each question in order.

1. Think of a leader . . .
2. Now write down the actual behaviors and actions that you have observed or are aware of that the person engaged in that support why you believe he or she is a leader . . .

Share your responses with a partner. Identify commonalities and differences in your responses.

Share out commonalities and differences with the full group. Identify themes in the responses.

Ask: Did anyone have trouble moving from question 1 to question 2? Why? When discussing leader and leadership, where do we place the preponderance of our focus? On the individual or on the process? Why is this so?

What if we switched the questions? Ask two new questions—again leaving time for responses for each.

1. Think of behaviors that lead you to want to work with someone . . .
2. Think of individuals who demonstrate these behaviors . . .

Share your responses with the same partner. Identify commonalities and differences in your responses.

Share out commonalities and differences with the full group. Identify themes in the responses.

Ask: What is the difference in the approaches of the two sets of questions? What is the result in our responses? What is the impact on how and who we see as potential leaders?

Close the activity with students talking with the same partner answering these two questions:

- I believe leadership is . . .
- I believe a leader is . . .

Activity 3: Responding to Reflection Prompts

Time: 25 minutes

Chapter 1 states that not only will you most likely find yourself reflected in this book but also that we develop best when we are open to learning. These reflective questions are designed to assist you in the reflective process of identifying your own paradigms around leadership and what you hope to learn from this experience.

Set up this reflection activity with a conversation on two of the reflection questions found in the back of Chapter 1. How might these two questions guide your learning over this program?

- What is your leadership purpose?
- How can knowing more about leadership make you more successful in your future endeavors?

Through reflection we can become experts of our experience. The following questions are designed to prompt reflection on the daily practices that shape your leadership knowing, doing, and being.

> Turning to One Another: Simple Conversations to Restore Hope to the Future

What beliefs motivate me to be interested in leadership?

How do I define the concepts of leader and leadership?

What actions do I notice in my relationships with others? In my group experiences?

What roles do I assume in groups?

What beliefs motivate me to assume these roles?

What kind of leader do I want to become?

My academic discipline provides me a unique lens for leadership because . . .

Role models who I learn from are . . .

My strengths are . . .

Within my relationships with others, how might I practice these strengths more?

I am guided by my core values of . . .

I stray from my values when . . .

What rituals or daily practices are important to me in my life?

When am I most likely experience moments of learning and growth?

What recent moments have I experienced that felt truly authentic . . . moments when I was my best self . . .

I am working toward...

I will know when I get there because...

As a result of participating in this leadership learning I hope to learn...

I have support for this learning from...

My first step will be...

Dr. Laura Osteen is the director of the Florida State University Center for Leadership and Social Change, where she loves learning with students through the university's undergraduate academic certificate in leadership studies.

Active Learning Module 1b

Exploring the Meaning of Leader and Follower

Aaron Asmundson

> Summary of Concepts

This learning module addresses a portion of Chapter 1, An Introduction to Leadership. In this section, students learn about the concept of the paradigm shift, and particularly the shift from focusing on the individual leader to examining leadership as a process among people. This has resulted in much more attention given to the role of group members or "followers" in the leadership process. In order to fully understand the relational leadership model, it is critical to understand this change in perspective.

The chapter explores this issue in two ways: first, through the concept of *followership*, which reimagines the important role of the follower; second, through the approach that would replace the term *follower* with a word that better expresses the reciprocal dynamic among group members in which influence goes both ways, such as *collaborator* or *co-creator*.

This section of the chapter concludes with a clarification that in *Exploring Leadership* (3rd edition), the term *leader* does not refer to the person holding a particular position of authority, but to any person engaged with others in the leadership process, regardless of his or her role within a hierarchy.

> Learning Outcomes

Students will

- Assess their own skills and capacities in regards to followership competencies
- Understand the influential role that followers play in supporting and defining leaders
- Consider the relevance of terms like *leader* and *follower* in a paradigm that sees leadership as a reciprocal relationship

> Module Overview

In this learning module, students explore the different positions, dynamics, roles, and relationships followers inhabit when working with leaders in a variety of sectors and styles. Specifically, this module will explore the concepts presented in Exhibit 1.1 of *Exploring Leadership* (3rd edition) concerning followership competencies.

Students engage in a small group discussion regarding the Five Follower Competencies in Exhibit 1.1. Through discussion, students will determine which competencies they think are strong determiners for their personal follower styles, identify areas for improvement, and generate questions for large group discussion regarding any concerns or confusion they have about these concepts.

Then, as an entire group, students view various pictures of famous or local leaders and are asked to respond as to the likelihood that they would want to "follow" these leaders if they were personally interacting with them in a group setting. Based on general reactions to each leader, students reflect on the characteristics of leaders they generally prefer to work with. In the final reflection, students explore the meaning of the term *follower* in the context of a reciprocal approach to leadership, such as the approach reflected in the relational leadership model.

Estimated Time

Activity 1: Small Group Discussion about the Five Follower
      Competencies, 20 minutes

Activity 2: Portraits of Leaders—Would I follow them and why?
      10-minute activity, 15-minute reflective discussion

Activity 3: Final Individual Reflection, 15 minutes

Materials/Supplies

Board or flip chart for any large group discussion points

Pen and paper for individual reflection

Pictures of various leaders that students recognize easily that
      generate strong opinions. (Global, national, and/or local
      community and campus leaders recognizable to all students in
      the group)

❯ Module Activities

Activity 1: Small Group Discussion about the Five Follower Competencies

Time: 15-minute reflective discussion in small groups, 5-minute discussion in large groups

In small groups (ideally no more than four people), instruct students to review Exhibit 1.1: Follower Competencies. Ask them to consider the following questions and engage in dialogue around them:

- Of the five competencies, which come easiest for you when working with others? Why is that?
- Which are most difficult? Why is this so?
- As a follower, which competencies best help determine the strength of connection you have to the leader that you're working with?
- Are there any that are confusing or that you need assistance in understanding fully?

Reconvene the students as a large group and ask for a few groups to share some of the main points of their discussion. Also, be sure to address the final question and allow time to clear up any confusion or questions about the competencies.

Activity 2: Portraits of Leaders—Would I follow them and why?

Time: 10-minute activity, 15-minute reflective discussion

Introduce this portion of the activity by pointing out that a large piece of leadership is behaving in a way that engages our followers in a way that "brings to life" each of the Five Follower Competencies being discussed. Therefore, as we continue to explore our capacities for leadership development, it is important to recognize what kinds of leadership traits and abilities welcome strong followership instead of suffocating it.

On a PowerPoint slideshow or flip chart, post pictures of leaders that are familiar faces and names to the group. Some possibilities might be national political leaders or people recently in the news for events related to their work and leadership decisions. Instruct participants to gain a sense of what they know about each leader shown and decide how willing they would be to "follow" these leaders if given the opportunity based on the Five Follower Competencies. For each competency regarding each leader, have them consider the following questions:

Displays loyalty	How committed would you be to the organization that this individual leads? Why or why not? How well does your personal vision fit with the vision of this leader?
Functions well in change-oriented environments	What opportunities are there to shift and adapt when working with this leader? Are there opportunities to lead as well as follow?
Functions well on teams	Do you see this leader providing a team-oriented environment? Are there opportunities for collaboration? Does this leader share credit with her or his team?
Thinks independently and critically	Are differences in opinion valued by this leader? What opportunities to act courageously can be rewarded by him or her?
Considers integrity of paramount importance	Does this leader generate a culture of mutual trust? How is honesty valued in this environment? What evidence is there of high performance standards?

After the individual assessment of each leader, have the group discuss their thoughts together:

- What leaders shown inspired you most to be a follower of them?
- Which leaders made you wary about following them?
- Which of the Five Follower Competencies stand out to you as particularly important for you when working with leaders? What does this teach you about the types of leaders to look for in your personal life?

- Generally, what does this exercise teach you about the relationship between leaders and followers? How are these relationships reciprocal or even interchangeable?

Activity 3: Final Individual Reflection

Time: 15 minutes

In the final reflection, students explore the meaning of the term *follower* in the context of an approach to leadership that focuses on the process of people working together in relationships that feature two-way influence. You may choose to have students share their thoughts with the large group if there is time.

Reflection questions to consider:

- What does this activity teach you about the influence of leader on followers? What about the influence of followers on leaders?
- As you think about the opportunities for leadership in your life, what role do you play in developing good followers? And what role do your followers play in developing your leadership?
- Where in your life are there opportunities to follow more intentionally? What is the difference between playing an active followership role and playing a leadership role? Is there a difference?
- Chapter 1 of *Exploring Leadership* (3rd edition) explored whether the terms *leader* and *follower* continue to be relevant in organizations where people work collaboratively and group members are empowered to participate in idea sharing and decision making. In such groups, in which multiple roles need to be filled in order to share the work, are terms like *collaborator* more accurate than *leader/follower*?

Variation   Depending on how well the group knows each other, consider replacing "famous" leaders with the leaders in the room or the participants themselves. This activity could be used as an opportunity to reflect on and establish some norms or change norms about the dynamic between leader and follower for all the participants involved. In turn, this activity could be used as an opportunity for participants to provide critical and positive feedback to each other about their own skills and competencies regarding followership.

Aaron Asmundson is the assistant director for Leadership Education and Development —Undergraduate Programs at the University of Minnesota. In this role, Aaron teaches courses in the undergraduate leadership minor and coordinates cocurricular leadership development programs.

Active Learning Module 2a

What Is Leadership?
Myths, Truths, and Definitions

Kristan Cilente Skendall

> Summary of Concepts

This learning module addresses Chapter 2 of *Exploring Leadership*, The Changing Nature of Leadership. In this section, students explore the myths, such as "leaders are born, not made," and truths of leadership. Further, the concepts of *leader* with *leadership* are contrasted in tracing the varied definitions of leadership over time. The section concludes with metaphorical definitions of leadership, such as leadership as jazz or whitewater.

> Learning Outcomes

Students will

- Be able to identify the myths and truths of relational leadership
- Understand the historical underpinnings of the concept of leadership
- Consider metaphorical approaches to leadership

> Module Overview

As a large group, students engage in conversations about the myths and truths of leadership by moving around a room to mark the level of agreement with a certain statement. Students then work in small groups to draw their definitions of leadership based upon the definitions and metaphors provided in the chapter. The module closes with the large group creating a unique musical experience to demonstrate the importance of each individual in leadership.

Estimated Time

Activity 1: Four Corners—Myths versus Truths, 15-minute activity, 5 minute reflective discussion

Activity 2: Draw the Leader(ship), 20-minute activity, 10-minute reflective discussion

Activity 3: Music Maker, 10-minute activity

Materials/Supplies

Signs for Four Corners (strongly agree, agree, strongly disagree, disagree)

Paper

Markers

Scissors

Tape

Glue

> Module Activities

Activity 1: Four Corners—Myths versus Truths

Time: 15-minute activity, 5-minute reflective discussion

In a room large enough for your group to move around, place the Signs for Four Corners (Strongly Agree, Agree, Strongly Disagree, Disagree) around the room (ideally, one in each corner).

Tell the students that they will have to choose one corner to describe the level with which they agree or disagree with each of the following statements. You may choose if you would like students to choose one corner or if they could be in the middle of two categories (if they could not decide if they strongly agreed or just agreed with a statement). Facilitators should let students know that they should go to the corner that best represents their opinion, not necessarily the views outlined in the book.

Once you go through the instructions, read each of the following statements. After you read each statement, allow students to move to the area of the room that represents their level of agreement. Before moving onto the next statement, once students have chosen their corner, ask someone from each group to defend his or her decision.

- Leaders are born, not made.
- Leadership is hierarchical, and you need to hold a formal position (have status and power) to be considered a leader.
- You have to have charisma to be an effective leader.
- There is one standard way of leading.
- It is impossible to be a manager and a leader at the same time.
- You only need to have common sense to be an effective leader.

After all statements have been read, bring the students back together for a large group debrief discussion. Topics will vary depending upon the level of agreement or disagreement among your group and between your students and the textbook. Some debriefing questions include

- Many of you chose views opposite of those expressed in the book. What would it take to change your views on leadership?
- There was much disagreement among the group regarding certain leadership beliefs. How might you come to work well together despite your varied views?
- There was much agreement among the group regarding certain leadership beliefs. What views might not be represented given the general consensus? Why would another perspective be important in a leadership discussion?

● Why should we discuss the myths of leadership? How does this connect with our group?

Activity 2: Draw the Leader(ship)

Time: 20-minute activity, 10-minute reflective discussion

Divide the students into small groups of three to four. Provide each small group with paper, markers, scissors, tape, and glue (these supplies can be altered based on your craft supplies).

Ask each group to illustrate their definition of leader(ship) based upon the many approaches defined in the chapter. Some students may define a leader, rather than leadership. It will be important to distinguish between these concepts, as the reciprocal leadership presented in the book is not about the "leader," but focuses on "leadership."

Once all small groups have completed their illustration, have each group present their product to the large group. Allow time for students to ask one another questions about their definitions.

Following the presentations and questions among the students, see if you can identify themes to create a meta-definition for the group. Conclude the activity with a brief discussion on the many ways in which being a leader and leadership have been defined; however, for the purpose of the book, the authors define leadership as "a relational and ethical process of people together attempting to accomplish positive change" (*Exploring Leadership*, 3rd edition).

Activity 3: Music Maker

Time: 10 minutes

To illustrate a metaphor of leadership, have the group stand in a large circle. The facilitator should stand in the middle of the circle and give the following instructions:

We will go around the circle and I will ask each person to make one unique noise. Each participant should continue to make that noise until I come to tell him or her to stop.

The facilitator will then choose one person who will start. That person could clap, snap, stomp feet, or make some other noise. The person should repeat that noise while you invite the person standing next to the initial noise-maker to make a different noise. Both people should continue until everyone is invited to make a noise to contribute to the group. Once everyone is performing some sort of noise, pause so that a unique piece of music has been created. Then, beginning with the first person, walk around the circle and instruct participates to stop making their noise individually until no one is making noise any longer.

The purpose of this activity is to illustrate how each person uniquely contributes to something larger than themselves. This is a metaphor for leadership and is a way to illustrate that with the entire group.

Variation   An alternative to this activity is the "Human Rain Storm," for which instructions can be found on the Internet.

> Facilitator Notes

The facilitator should consider the purpose of his or her group as the context for these activities. The "Four Corners" debrief may vary depending upon the context for the group engaging in the activity.

Kristan Cilente Skendall is the associate director of the Gemstone Program in the Honors College at the University of Maryland, College Park. Kristan received her PhD in the College Student Personnel Program at the University of Maryland in 2012. Her research focused on the relationship between short-term service immersion participation and socially responsible leadership.

Active Learning Module 2b

Generations of Leadership Theory

Michelle L. Kusel

> ## Summary of Concepts

This learning module addresses Chapter 2, The Changing Nature of Leadership. In this section, the authors set the foundation for the importance of understanding the purpose of leadership: leadership for what purpose? Equally important, the authors explain approaches and theories to understand the *how* of leadership.

Students explore the different thoughts of leadership from both the industrial and postindustrial eras. The chapter covers a variety of leadership approaches, including the great man approach, trait approaches, behavior approaches, situational contingency, influence, chaos theories, and reciprocal leadership approaches.

> ## Learning Outcomes

Students will

- Be able to articulate how and where they recognize different leadership theories and approaches

- Consider ways in which they see leadership approaches and theories present in their own leadership style
- Reflect on their personal perceptions and interpretations of different leadership theories and approaches

> Module Overview

Students view video clips from a variety of movies and discuss where they saw a leadership theory or approach in the film, how they see the theory present or absent from their leadership style, and express their opinion of the theory or approach and its practicality. These discussions can take place as a large group or in smaller pairs or triads, depending on group size.

Estimated Time

Each film clip varies in length so the total time needed can vary depending on which movie clips are chosen to be shown. If all clips are shown, the module will need approximately 90 minutes to complete.

Materials/Supplies

Technology to project online video clips

Board or flip charts with markers to write down points emerging from discussion

Movie clips (find detailed information and relevant links for each clip)

> Module Activities

Activity 1: Movie Clips and Discussion

Explain to students that this activity is about examining leadership theories and approaches through the use of film. As they watch the video clips, they should take notes about how they witnessed the theory or approach in the clip.

[Show clip]

Have students break into pairs or triads to discuss the leadership they noticed in these clips, along with how they see the theory in action in their life and their opinions on the validity of the theory. Then have the groups share their primary points to the larger group.

In the larger group, also ask the following questions after each clip to engage in discussion with different students. These questions are from Chapter Two of *Exploring Leadership* (3rd edition).

- Does anyone relate to this theory or metaphor to best describe your leadership approach? Why?
- What motivates you to take on leadership responsibilities or roles and why? Why do you lead?

[Show next clip and repeat the process]

Movie Clips

Great Man Approach   Play the clip from *Tron* (2010) that takes place in the son's apartment after he has pulled a prank at the large company his father owned. The son asks the family friend, "Do I look like a leader?" to which the friend responds, "No." Queue movie to 15:31 and end at 16:26.

Trait Approach   Play the clip from *The Princess Bride* (1987) that discusses a contest of wits where one man has to decide from which cup to drink. Queue movie to 29:35 and end at 34:37.

Behavioral Approach   Play a clip from the movie *Office Space* (1999) in which the main character is asked to work the weekend. Queue the movie to 19:00 and end at 20:47. This clip is also available on YouTube, titled "Office Space—Working Tomorrow."

Situational Contingency Approaches   Play the clip from *The Blind Side* (2009) in which the mother goes onto the field to tell Michael that the football team is like his family and he has to protect them. This clip is also available on YouTube, titled "blindside p and p 2."

Influence Theories   Play the clip from *Dead Poet's Society* (1989) where the students rebel and stand on their desks proclaiming "Oh captain, my captain." This clip is also available on YouTube, titled "Dead Poets Society."

Transforming Leadership Theory   Play the clip from *Remember the Titans* (2000) in which the coach tells the players about the battle of Gettysburg. This clip is also available on YouTube, titled "Remember the Titans Coach Boone Speech."

Complexity Leadership Theory   Play the trailer to the movie *Pay It Forward* (2001). This is a good summary of the purpose of the film. It is available on YouTube, titled "Pay It Forward Trailer."

Adaptive Leadership   Play the clip from *Harry Potter and the Sorcerer's Stone* (2002) in which Ron (chess), Harry (flying), and Hermione (untangling the plants) all take turns solving a part of the puzzle to find their way. Queue movie to 1:56:35 and end at 2:02:05.

Shared Leadership   Play the clip from *Lord of the Rings: Fellowship of the Ring* (2001) in which the fellowship is formed to begin the journey to Mordor. Queue movie to 1:31:16 and end at 1:33:24.

Servant Leadership   Play the clip from *Star Trek* (2009) in which the captain sacrifices his life for the well-being of all on his ship in the beginning of the film. This is also the scene where Jim is born. Queue movie to 7:28 and end at 11:15.

> Facilitator Notes

There is much flexibility available with this module depending on time limitations. Each movie clip runs independently of the others and can be omitted or replaced with other content without disrupting the module.

Michelle L. Kusel is the Academic Internship Program manager at Loyola University Chicago.

Active Learning Module 2c

Emerging Leadership Theory

Wendy Wagner

> Summary of Concepts

This learning module addresses a portion of Chapter 2, The Changing Nature of Leadership. In this section, students explore the paradigm shift represented by newer leadership theories. Industrial era leadership theories were individualistic. They focused on the leader and goal achievement and assumed linear paths to change.

The postindustrial era has a reciprocal leadership approach. These new and emerging theories give attention to the roles of every group member. A positive group process is as important as goal achievement. Problems are understood to have multiple, interrelated causes and solutions.

> Learning Outcomes

Students will

- Be able to articulate the differences between industrial and postindustrial (or reciprocal) leadership approaches

- Consider which of these emerging approaches are a good fit for various contexts and why
- Have a foundation upon which to truly appreciate and understand the elements of the relational leadership model

› Module Overview

Students view video clips of musical performances. One is a classical piece by a traditional orchestra and one is a familiar standard by an improvisational jazz band. The subsequent discussion considers these performances as metaphors for the many differences between the industrial and postindustrial/reciprocal leadership approaches.

Students then discuss their own leadership context in terms of these metaphors, and explore what the new and emerging postindustrial leadership models would look like in those contexts.

Estimated Time
Activity 1: Orchestra versus Improv Jazz, 10-minute viewing videos, 30-minute discussion
Activity 2: Connection to Theory, 10-minute directed discussion
Activity 3: Connection to Experience, 10-minute small group discussion

Materials/Supplies
Technology to project online video clips

Board or flip charts with markers to write down points emerging from discussion

A video clip of a traditional orchestra, playing a familiar classical piece

One example: http://www.youtube.com/watch?v=2eTlaE5y9hk

A video clip of an improvisational jazz group, playing a familiar jazz standard

One example: http://www.youtube.com/watch?v=4k-uUr0BmS4
For those less familiar with improvisational jazz, the following
video clip includes an explanation of how the musicians work
together: http://www.youtube.com/watch?v=bMPvbr_647M&
feature=relmfu

> Module Activities

Activity 1: Orchestra versus Improv Jazz

Time: 40 minutes

Explain to students that this activity is about examining two
types of musical traditions as examples of different approaches to
leadership. As they watch the two video clips, they should take
notes about everything they notice related to leadership in this
context.

Play the two video clips, for at least five minutes each.

In small groups, have students discuss the leadership they
noticed in these clips, then have the groups share their primary
points to the larger group.

Play the two video clips again. Before the second viewing,
ask students to consider each as a metaphor for leadership
approaches in other settings, like student organizations. Suggest
the following specific points if they haven't already surfaced in
the initial discussion.

- Whose goal is it? Who decides what will be done and how?
- What is the division of labor? Who takes direction from
  whom?
- What is the nature of the relationships among the musicians?
- How is the context different? What is the audience expecting
  in each?

Debriefing Questions

- What are the differences between the two musical groups in terms of the four questions above?
- Has anyone been in a musical group? Describe your experience as a group member in that context.
- What is the role of context in each, and how do these affect the leadership approaches used?
  - Orchestra: more formal setting, the audience expects the song to be played exactly as the composer wrote it, a much larger number of musicians, performers are in fixed positions facing the conductor . . .
  - Improv band: looser rules about propriety for audience and performers, the song is familiar but the audience expects a creative, unique take on it, only a few performers, performers face each other, move around, audience participation (clapping or singing along is typical) . . .
- How does context affect group dynamics and leadership in other settings?
  - Size of group (small team vs. hundreds vs. thousands connected virtually)
  - Goal of group (need for precision in execution like a military endeavor or factory production of computer components vs. need for empowerment to make unique contributions such as a civil rights movement or creative endeavor)
- What leadership settings fit the orchestra allegory in terms of the nature of the goal, context, and leadership approach? What setting fit the improvisational band approach? *Military and industrial organizations are typically suggested as being similar to the large size, precision, and top-down leadership approach of an orchestra. Civil rights movements, many student organizations, creative fields like marketing and theater are cited as more like an improv band.*

- What is the experience of the participants in each musical group? Do you have a preferred type of group you'd like to be in? Which would bring out the best in you?

Activity Variation   Comparing a scripted play to improvisational comedy is another useful analogy. A guest speaker can be brought in to more fully explain some of the basic techniques of improvisational comedy. These techniques are easily comparable to postindustrial/reciprocal leadership approaches.

Optional   The following short video clip features the chair of a software company discussing the changing nature of the workplace and the need to move from a "marching band" metaphor to an "improv jazz" metaphor. http://www.youtube.com/watch?v=1LJhJFEKrkc

Activity 2: Connection to Theory

Time: 10 minutes

Discuss connections to the *Exploring Leadership* reading:

- As leadership studies began as a field of academic study, research was primarily conducted in military and industrial settings. Emerging models are often reflective of other settings.
  - Would a theory based on research in one context be useful in another? There isn't a right answer here—some aspects are transferrable, some aren't. Encourage students to consider how to be discerning about new theories they encounter in order to take what is useful and question what might not be useful.
- If you have already discussed the leadership theory families, discuss which families resemble an orchestra and which resemble an improv band.
- Discuss the concept of paradigm shifts and how the shift from industrial to postindustrial represents a whole set of issues rather than a simple shift in style.

- Discuss the concept of followership and its connection to the postindustrial paradigm.
- Discuss the "Leadership Maps for a Rapidly Changing World" section of the chapter. Which musical style is more aligned with the linear approach? Which is in alignment with the description of "order without predictability" of chaos theory? (Consider the adherence to the written music vs. the free interpretation of the jazz standard.) The concept of the melody line in the jazz standard as an example of a "pattern" is relevant here.
- The reading explores the many ways that modern organizations operate in an environment different from that in previous decades. What does that context mean for what is needed from leaders? Do the students agree that today's complexity, constant change, and ambiguity require leaders who can improvise? What does improvisation look like in an organizational context?
- The reading emphasizes the importance of relationships in leadership. How is the nature of those relationships different in the two music metaphors (including relationships between leader and member and members with each other)?

Activity 3: Connection to Experience

Time: 10 minutes

In pairs or small groups, have students discuss the following:

- What is your leadership context? Which musical form is it most like? Discuss exactly why you think so.
- Which paradigm is more like your preferred approach to leadership? Has that been a fit for your context?
- What would the orchestra conductor approach look like in your organization—in what ways would it be effective and not be effective? What about the improv band approach?

> Facilitator Notes

Be prepared for a wide range of leadership issues to surface here. This can be a great day to revisit in subsequent workshops or courses, as it provides common language for a host of complex ideas that emerge as students gain a deeper understanding of leadership issues.

Wendy Wagner is an assistant professor of leadership and community engagement at George Mason University. She is also the director of Mason's Center for Leadership and Community Engagement.

Active Learning Module 3a

The Relational Leadership Model

Sean Gehrke

> Summary of Concepts

This learning module addresses Chapter 3, The Relational Leadership Model. This chapter presents a model for understanding leadership as *a relational and ethical process of people together attempting to accomplish positive change*. Relationships are the focal point of this definition. The chapter discusses five primary components of leadership as being

- Purposeful
- Inclusive
- Empowering
- Ethical
- Process-oriented

In order to practice relational leadership, students must be knowledgeable of key processes, aware of how these processes affect themselves and others, and act on this awareness and knowledge. The knowing-being-doing model provides a useful heuristic for students to apply the components of relational leadership to their groups and communities.

> Learning Outcomes

Students will

- Explore their personal conceptions of leadership and how they relate to the relational leadership model
- Understand the five components of the relational leadership model
- Apply the components the relational leadership model to their personal contexts and communities

> Module Overview

This module is designed to move quickly through the relational leadership model and its five components. It involves a facilitator-led discussion of the definition of relational leadership, followed by five fast-paced, interactive activities and discussions designed to introduce the students to the five components of relational leadership and apply them to a specific community or context.

Estimated Time

Activity 1: Introduction to Relational Leadership: 10 minutes

Activity 2: Purpose, 2-minute introduction by facilitator, 8-minute small group discussion

Activity 3: Empowering, 2-minute introduction by facilitator, 8-minute small group discussion

Activity 4: Inclusive, 2- minute introduction by facilitator, 8-minute small group discussion

Activity 5: Ethical, 2-minute introduction by facilitator, 8-minute small group discussion

Activity 6: Process, 6-minute small group activity, 2-minute definition by facilitator

Closing remarks: 2 minutes

Materials/Supplies

Board or flip charts with markers to write down leadership definition and fill in relational leadership model.

> Module Activities

Prior to beginning this module, write the following definition of leadership on the flip chart and cover it up with a second piece of paper from the flip chart: *Leadership is a relational and ethical process of people together attempting to accomplish positive change.* Also, draw the outline of the relational leadership model (Figure 3.1 in *Exploring Leadership*, 3rd edition), but do not fill in the words; you will fill these in as you progress through the module.

Activity 1: Introduction to Relational Leadership

Time: 10 minutes

Begin by asking for a few students to volunteer an answer to the following questions:

- Who here thinks they are a good leader? (*ask for show of hands*) What reasons do they have for thinking so?
- What have you learned about leadership, either at college, in the community, or elsewhere?

Reveal the definition of leadership previously written on the flip chart. Highlight specific words or phrases that stand out to you as setting this definition of leadership apart from conceptions that students revealed in the initial discussion, such as "process," "people together," and "attempting to accomplish positive change." Underlying these aspects of the definition can help with this discussion.

Briefly introduce knowing-being-doing as the three principles for engaging in relational leadership. Define what you mean by each:

- *Knowing*: You must know—yourself, how change occurs, and how and why others may view things differently than you do.
- *Being (attitude)*: You must be—ethical, principled, open, caring, and inclusive.
- *Doing*: You must act—in socially responsible ways, consistently and congruently, as a participant in a community, and on your commitments and passions (quoted from *Exploring Leadership*, 2nd edition, pp. 5–6).

Activity 2: Purpose

Time: 10 minutes

Begin by splitting the group into smaller groups of four students each. Students will remain in these groups for the remainder of the activities.

Write "Purpose" in the middle circle of the model outline you drew on the flip chart, and provide a brief definition of relational leadership as purposeful, including

- Commitment to a goal or activity, collaborating, and finding common ground with others
- Purpose is at the core of leadership
- Purpose is essentially about vision—there are two types:
  - Personalized—Imposed by an individual on a group
  - Socialized—Built from among members of the entire group; everyone is involved in building it
- Importance of being purposefully committed to a vision for a group and for all members to articulate the purpose and use it as a driving force

- Highlight knowing-being-doing principles for purpose:
  - Knowing—Insight into own purpose, action
  - Being—Attitude of hope, ability to commit
  - Doing—Setting goals, motivating

In their small groups, have each student choose a group of which they are a member. This could be a student organization, sports team, residential community, team of coworkers, or any other group to which they belong. Have them discuss answers to the following questions related to the group they chose:

- What is the purpose/vision of your group?
- Do other members of your group know this vision? Can they articulate it?
- How can you ensure buy-in to this purpose?

Activity 3: Empowering

Time: 10 minutes

Write "Empowering" in the top right circle of model outline you drew on the flip chart, and provide a brief definition of relational leadership as empowering, including

- Consisting of two dimensions
  - Sense of self claiming ownership and expecting to be involved
  - Environment that promotes participation
- Five sources of power (we use these at different times, and some—coercive in particular—are often less appropriate than others)
  - Expert power—Information or knowledge
  - Referent power—Strength of relationship (e.g., elder)
  - Legitimate power—Positional role

- Coercive power—Threats of action or inaction
- Reward power—Positive outcome leads to desired resources
- Empowerment is not delegation
- Highlight knowing-being-doing principles for empowering:
  - Knowing—Understand power and influence; self-knowledge and self-esteem
  - Being—Committed to others;
  - Doing—Share proper information, bring people in

In their small groups, have students discuss answers to the following questions:

- Think of a time when you felt empowered in a group and a time when you did not feel empowered in a group. How did these two experiences affect your ability to interact within the group?
- What was the difference in group leadership and context between those two times?

Activity 4: Inclusive

Time: 10 minutes

Write "Inclusive" in the top left circle of the model outline you drew on the flip chart, and provide a brief definition of relational leadership as inclusive, including

- Understanding, valuing, and actively engaging diversity in group, including differing views, approaches, styles, and aspects of individuality
- Unity of many parts (i.e., individuals) is essential
- Connects to previous components
  - Building a shared purpose by utilizing differences of diverse groups
  - Developing members in order to empower them

- Inclusiveness is communicated through organizational practices and customs
- Important to be inclusive of stakeholders that are both internal and external to the group
- Highlight knowing-being-doing principles for inclusive:
  - Knowing—Understanding people, getting to know individuality of members
  - Being—Valuing involvement, equity
  - Doing—Listening, civil discourse

In their small groups, have students discuss answers to the following questions:

- Have you ever witnessed exclusion in a group? What were the consequences of this exclusion?
- What could have changed in the group to ensure inclusion was practiced?

Activity 5: Ethical

Time: 10 minutes

Write "Ethical" in the bottom center circle of the model outline you drew on the flip chart, and provide a brief definition of relational leadership as ethical, including

- Leadership driven by values and standards
- Relational leadership is good—moral—in nature
- Distinguish between ethical and moral:
  - Ethical—Group standards that govern behavior
  - Moral—Right versus wrong, good means to good ends
- Involves leading by example—Congruency between values and actions
- Highlight knowing-being-doing principles for ethical:
  - Knowing—Beliefs, values, and principles
  - Being—Worthy of trust
  - Doing—Confronting unethical practices

This activity occurs in two parts. First, have students generate individual lists of up to 10 values they feel define them as individuals. It is often helpful to provide examples of some values—such as honesty, integrity, hard work—when asking students to do this. Once they have settled on an initial list, ask them to identify the four or five values that they consider to be most important, or core, to them as individuals. They may protest that all of their values are core values. Be prepared to discuss with them that while all of their values are important, this exercise is designed to have them identify the values that are closest to their cores as individuals. Once they have settled on their core values, ask each group to pretend they are starting a new group and to use the core values they identified for themselves to generate a list of only three or four core values for the group they are about to form. Emphasize that this should be done by consensus. You will likely find that choosing their core values is not too difficult, but attempting to identify core values to guide their group is much more difficult. Facilitate a very brief discussion with the group after this exercise, or utilize the following prompts as things for the students to think about if you have no time for a discussion:

- Was it easy or difficult to settle on core values through consensus?
- How might you identify core values of the groups you belong to?
- How often might values conflicts occur in groups?

Activity Variation   If you feel like you have flexibility in time and would like to spend more time on the ethical activity, have students create longer initial lists of values (as many as 15 or 20), and then have them slowly whittle down the list to their core values in steps (e.g., now choose your 10 core values; now choose your seven core values). Allowing the students to list more values and be forced to identify core values from them is a way to illustrate how difficult it can be to identify one's own core values.

Activity 6: Process

Time: 10 minutes

Begin this activity with a small-group activity. In their small groups, ask students to quickly plan a community service project. After two minutes, stop the groups and ask for volunteers to report, not about what project they identified, but on the process they engaged in to plan the activity. Students are generally more used to reporting about the outcome of a group exercise and not as much about the process the group engaged in. Some helpful prompts for this brief discussion include

- How did your group identify which project to plan?
- Did each member of the group participate?
- Were you intentional about how you should engage in this activity, or was it basically a free-for-all of thoughts and ideas?

Write "Process" in the outer circle of the model outline you drew on the flip chart, and provide a brief definition of relational leadership as process-oriented, including

- How a group goes about being a group, sustains as a group, and meets its purpose
- Process involves recruitment and involvement of members, group decision making, and handling tasks related to mission and vision
- Processes must be intentionally designed for groups to function effectively
- Emphasize cooperation and collaboration

- Highlight knowing-being-doing principles for process:
  - Knowing—How process influences outcomes, understanding systems perspectives
  - Being—Value process
  - Doing—Group reflection, civil confrontation

Remind the group that this module was designed as a quick introduction to relational leadership and its five components. Let them know it was intentionally planned for them to quickly engage with the different aspects of leadership, and that future modules will delve into these components in depth.

> Facilitator Notes

As you can see, this module is designed to cover a lot of ground in a relatively short time. It is essential that you exercise strict time management in order to progress through all the activities in 60 minutes. Of course, if you end up with more time to deliver this module, you may prolong any of the activities as you see fit. You are likely to find that the students feel they were not given enough time to fully engage with a particular component—this is good! Remind them that this module serves only as an introduction and that you hope it is whetting their appetites, so to speak, to learn more about the relational leadership model.

Sean Gehrke is a Dean's Fellow pursuing his PhD in higher education at the University of Southern California. He is a researcher in the Pullias Center for Higher Education, whose research focuses on social networks, faculty culture, and spirituality in higher education.

Active Learning Module 3b

Being Purposeful

Paul Stonecipher

> Summary of Concepts

This learning module addresses the "Being Purposeful" portion of Chapter 3, The Relational Leadership Model. Being purposeful is defined as "having a commitment to a goal or activity" requiring the "ability to collaborate and to find common ground." A socialized vision of what the group is working toward or hoping to achieve is the idea of establishing purpose. This requires the development of a shared vision of how the group or organization will contribute to improving the human condition in such a way that no intentional harm results.

> Learning Outcomes

Students will
- Be able to construct a socialized vision
- Develop their ability to collaborate on a purpose or vision statement
- Consider how to write a vision statement that supports positive change

> Module Overview

In a group setting, students are guided to develop purposeful vision statements under the guidelines of the Relational Leadership Model. Students collaborate as a team to develop a socialized vision that is purposeful and supports positive change.

Students then evaluate vision statements in terms of being purposeful and connected to the other four components of the Relational Leadership Model. Students carefully consider the construction of the vision statement and what possible outcomes of such a vision statement could be.

Estimated Time

Activity 1: Personalized to Socialized Vision

- Identification of stakeholders and consideration of interests: 5 minutes
- Development of socialized vision: 10 minutes
- Reporting and analysis: 5 minutes

Activity 2: Visionary Magazine Article

- Identify organization, mission/purpose, and media outlet: 5 minutes
- Develop article: 10 minutes
- Class presentation and discussion: 5 minutes

Activity 3: Develop a Vision Based on Values

- Identify the organizational values: 5 minutes
- Develop a vision to promote positive change: 10 minutes
- Individualized reflection: 5 minutes

Materials/Supplies

Examples of organization's mission or vision statements

A variety of magazines and trade publications, related to the selected organizations if possible

When searching for mission statements, you may wish to visit www.missionstatements.com/fortune_500_mission_statements.html which provides mission statements from

Fortune 500 companies as well as brief descriptions of what services that organization provides and current slogans.

> Module Activities

Activity 1: Personalized to Socialized Vision

Time: 20 minutes

Begin by selecting a preestablished vision statement. Such statements can come from nationally recognized corporations, nonprofit organizations, or can even be the mission statement of students' school, college, or university.

Ask the students to identify possible stakeholders. Then assign groups of students to represent the views or interests of the stakeholders identified. In the example of the universities, students would take on the roles and interests of faculty, the university president and other administrators, alumni, students, and so forth. Then, having assumed those stakeholders' roles, students should work together to socially transform the original vision statement. Remind students that the statement should be purposeful and able to guide the next four elements of the Relational Leadership Model. The statement should also promote positive change. Give them 10 minutes to complete this step.

Upon completion of the statement or when time is up, facilitate an evaluation of the group's accomplishments and individual experiences:

- Were all voices heard and incorporated into the statement? Were any stakeholders left out; if so, why?
- What expectations did they use to define the goal of "promoting positive change?"
- How does this statement contribute to improving the human condition?
- How much different is this statement from the original personalized statement?

- How well does the resulting statement contribute to the next four elements of the Relational Leadership Model? Is there clear direction given for focusing the action of the organization as a result of the socialized statement?

Activity 2: Visionary Magazine Article

Time: 20 minutes

Provide students a variety of handouts identifying an organization and its mission and vision statements. Divide the students into smaller groups and have them select one of these organizations. The group will develop the content for a feature article in a news magazine or trade publication that will describe the organization as if we had jumped five or ten years into the future, looking back on where that vision statement had brought the organization. Have a group member present the article to the full group. Facilitate discussion of how they came to that projection of the future.

- Challenge groups to directly tie the article's depiction of the organization to the mission or vision statement.
- Can the larger group of students envision that future based on the statement and the small group presentation?
- Is the presentation believable? Were the presenters overly optimistic about the organization based on the vision or mission statement or do the students buy into this vision of the future?
- What challenges did the presenting group experience based on the vision statements? How hard was it for them to envision the future?

Variations   Given more time or the opportunity for prework, you may allow students to select their own organizations and bring the mission and vision statements with them to the session.

Given more time, another variation is to provide each group with a camera and allow them to develop a television news presentation covering the growth and development of the organization and what it has accomplished in the last five to ten years. Students could then present these in class.

Activity 3: Develop a Vision Based on Values

Time: 20 minutes

This is an opportunity for the students to develop a vision statement from scratch based on their operational and end values. End values are essential conceptualizations of what the future would look like or the ultimate goals of an organization such as freedom, health, or equality. Operational values are those values the organization believes are essential or important to achieve the established end goals; for example, honesty, loyalty, or compassion.

Divide the students into small groups. In each group, students should think of an organization (for example, a student organization, nonprofit organization, or neighborhood association) and then designate three end and operational values for that organization. Based on those values, have the students develop a purposeful vision statement that promotes positive change. Challenge them further to remember the other elements of the Relational Leadership Model in the development of the vision statement.

Have the groups present the resulting vision statements, clarifying what their organization was as well as the values they began with. Then provide the students the opportunity to reflect on the experience.

- How and why did they come up with the values they did? Did they feel any values were missing or overlooked by their group?
- Did they feel the final vision statement reflected the values established?
- How would they feel about working for an organization with that vision statement?

> Facilitator Notes

This is a great opportunity to bring other conversations together or to set up activities that can be carried forward into other discussions. Also, feel free to play "devil's advocate" through the conversations and challenge the students to think through lenses different from those they are accustomed to. For example, ask how their vision statements and efforts might work for a different culture or even another country.

Paul Stonecipher is a doctoral student in higher education at Florida State University and program coordinator for an online certificate in institutional research. He also is an instructor in the university's undergraduate certificate in leadership studies, teaching leadership theory and practice.

Active Learning Module 3c

Being Inclusive

Tom Segar

> Summary of Concepts

This learning module addresses the "Being Inclusive" portion of Chapter 3, The Relational Leadership Model. Students explore the importance of valuing diverse perspectives and beliefs of all group members and how embracing diversity can lead to more mutually beneficial outcomes.

Inclusive leaders seek to incorporate the input of all shareholders and stakeholders, particularly individuals whose voices sometimes go unheard. They realize that existing processes for participation may be exclusive of others. Therefore, they actively seek the contributions of all group members and others outside of the group who may experience the impact of the group's decision.

> Learning Outcomes

Students will

- Be able to articulate leadership practices that demonstrate inclusiveness

- Consider the impact of inclusive and exclusive practices on group outcomes
- Have the capacity to name personal strategies for incorporating inclusiveness

> Module Overview

The students participate in a two-part process of exploring inclusive behavior. First, students use three multicolored pipe cleaners to answer the question, "Who are you?" After participants share their creations the instructor presents a transparent, eight-ounce measuring cup and asks participants, "Who thinks they can fit themselves into my cup?" Participants provide varying responses, and the instructor facilitates a discussion about how the cup can be a barrier to inclusiveness.

Finally, the instructor assembles the students into two groups uneven in size and provides each with different instructions. Students use Play-Doh™ or another modeling compound to shape several creations to represent inclusive campus environments. Following the simulation, each group presents their creations and debriefs the activity.

Estimated Time
Activity 1: Individual Dimensions of Inclusion
- Individual activity: 5 minutes
- Paired sharing: 5 minutes
- Directed discussion: 20 minutes

Activity 2: Group Dimensions of Inclusion
- Group activity: 15 minutes
- Directed discussion: 20 minutes

Materials/Supplies
Three multicolored pipe cleaners per participant
One eight-ounce, transparent, measuring cup

12 cans of Play-Doh™ or generic modeling compound

Wax paper or similar materials to cover table top

Board or flip charts with markers to write down points emerging from discussion

> Module Activities

Activity 1: Individual Dimensions of Inclusion

Time: 30 minutes

Explain to students that this activity is a personal exploration into how they see themselves. Distribute three multicolored pipe cleaners to each student. Ask students to answer the question, "Who are you?" using the pipe cleaners. Students can shape the pipe cleaners in any fashion that they choose to answer this question. Encourage students to go beyond sharing basic data such as their class year and major. Remind students that there are no incorrect answers to this question, and their creations should simply speak to how they see themselves.

As students finish shaping their pipe cleaners, invite them to share their creations with one or two other students. Invite them to articulate how what they made says who they are, and why they choose to express themselves in that way.

Present the measuring cup to the students and pose the question, "Who believes they can fit their creation into this measuring cup?" Spend a minute or two allowing students to attempt to fit their creations into the cup. Ask for a show of hands of students who cannot fit their creations into the cup.

Facilitate a directed discussion with the following questions.

• What if your worthiness to be part of a group or to participate in a leadership process was determined based on your ability to fit into the cup?

• Should you have to change who you are to fit into the cup?

- Who gets left out of the cup and why?
- Is the cup an accurate measure of one's worthiness?
- What might the cup represent?
- How might our organizations impose the cup unfairly on others?
- What are some ways we can address the unfair application of the cup to others?

Conclude the discussion by asking participants to consider the unconscious ways they may impose "the cup" on others, and how they may work individually and within groups to dismantle the cup.

Activity 2: Group Dimensions of Inclusion

Time: 35 minutes

Explain to the students that they will be participating in an experiential activity in which they will need to create several objects based on instructions the facilitator will provide. Divide the students into two groups with one-third of the students in one group and two-thirds of the students in the other group. Place the groups on opposite sides of the room away from one another.

Provide the small group with eight cans of Play-Doh™ and share the following instructions.

- Please use the Play-Doh™ provided to create a representation of what a welcoming and inclusive campus community would look and feel like.
- Make sure everyone in the group has a voice and has the opportunity to contribute to the process.
- Work collaboratively to complete the project.
- Feel free to be as creative as you want—have fun!
- Remind the group they will have 15 minutes to complete their project.

Next, provide the large group with four cans of Play-Doh™ and share the following instructions.

- Please use the Play-Doh™ provided to create a representation of what a welcoming and inclusive campus community would look and feel like.
- Only one person will be the leader and spokesperson of the group.
- The group leader will decide how to best design and complete the project.
- Group members must follow the directions of the leader.
- Remind the group that they will have 15 minutes to complete the project.

Directed Discussion   Ask each the small group to present their project first. Then, ask the group leader of the large group to present the large group's project. Thank both groups for their work and invite them to return to their seats. Next, invite members of the large group to describe their experience working on the project. Then invite members of the small group to describe their experience working on the project. After processing student responses about their group experiences, begin asking the following questions:

Discussion Questions
- How would you describe the difference between the experiences of the small and large group?
- How would you compare the difference in outcomes between the small and large group?
- If you were in the large group, what challenges did you experience?
- If you were in the small group, what challenges did you experience?
- How might this activity reflect what happens in real groups?

- What could have been done differently to facilitate a more inclusive experience for the large group?
- What meaning do you make of the different amount of resources, both human and physical, provided to each group?
- What strategies can be used in the future to create a more inclusive process for all involved?

Help the group identify leadership practices that demonstrate inclusiveness by noting the difference in leadership between the small and large group. As the group discusses the experiences in the large and small group, note the difference in the outcome between the two groups. Additional resources and a more inclusive approach are most likely to lead to a richer outcome.

> Facilitator Notes

Each activity in this module can be presented in two separate sessions. Focus on the discussion questions and participant comments more than the simulations.

Groups larger than 20 students may require more Play-Doh™ for Activity 2. As long as the ratio of materials is the same between the small and large groups, more Play-Doh™ is acceptable.

Dr. Thomas Segar is the vice president for student affairs at Shepherd University, where he also serves as an associate graduate professor in the College Student Development and Administration program. He received his PhD in college student personnel with a concentration in teaching and social justice from the University of Maryland.

Active Learning Module 3d

Being Empowering

Steve Mills

> Summary of Concepts

This learning module addresses the "Being Empowering" portion of Chapter 3, The Relational Leadership Model. This section explains that relational leadership is necessarily empowering, and it examines both the personal and contextual factors related to power that release and inhibit leadership potential. The chapter explores the role of power in leadership, covering the various sources of power, power assumptions, self-empowerment, and empowering environments.

> Learning Outcomes

Students will

- Consider the internal and external factors that encourage and inhibit their leadership voice
- Consider the role of formal power and the impact of designated leadership

- Understand the practical importance of empowered, individual input from everyone in a decision-making group
- Consider the role of leadership in providing the conditions necessary for a group to meet its potential

> Module Overview

Students experience an abrupt leadership vacuum in their group that must be filled according to the power-based leadership options they are willing to explore. Students consider their own self-empowerment and the personal and environmental factors that impact leadership in a peer group.

Students experience the factors necessary for groups to consistently perform better than the smartest person in the group. These factors (diverse members, independent input, and efficient aggregation of group input) are applied to a simple guessing game. Through this activity students consider the importance of empowering each member of a group and explore techniques for assuring that everyone's voice is heard in the decision-making process.

Estimated Time
Activity 1: Leaderless! 20-minute group activity, 20-minute discussion
Activity 2: The Wisdom of Crowds, 7-minute group activity, 13-minute discussion

Materials/Supplies
Scrap paper
Pens or pencils
Calculator

> Module Activities

Activity 1: Leaderless!

Time: 40 minutes

Group Activity   *Time*: 20 minutes

This activity is most effective when students and the group leader are seated in one large circle. The group leader makes sure she has everyone's attention, and states, "Your task, for the next 20 minutes, is to explore how leadership is given, received, and exercised in this group." After this point the group leader doesn't utter another word for 20 minutes, and continues to look straight ahead with a neutral expression on her face, even when addressed directly by the group.

Typically group members, with much nervous laughter, will settle into an anxiety-ridden process of attempting to follow the instructions without formal leadership present. They may demand more explicit instructions from the leader, *who must not respond in any way*. This forces group members to examine their own self-authority, and how they perceive their own sources of power in a leadership vacuum. Insightful group members will recognize the connection between the question they are exploring and the process they are experiencing.

Debriefing Questions   *Time*: 20 minutes

- What did you experience during this activity?
- What did you observe during this activity?
- What did you notice about the way authority was granted to leaders in this group?
- What sources of power were honored? (Encourage students to consider patterns they may be loath to recognize, such as power accorded due to gender, age, or race.)

- What external, environmental factors encouraged or inhibited your leadership voice?
- What personal, internal factors encouraged or inhibited your leadership voice?
- What insights have you gained related to the role of positional authority and formal power?

Activity 2: The Wisdom of Crowds

Time: 20 minutes

Group Activity   *Time*: 7 minutes

Begin by passing around a clear glass container full of a small, countable item such as marbles, puzzle pieces, or peppermint balls. You will have counted these items and will know the total. Give the students the following instructions: "When you receive this container, look it over quickly and record your best guess of the total number of [marbles] it holds on a scrap piece of paper. Do *not* share your guess with anyone and do *not* let anyone see what you have written. Keep your written guess folded on your desk until it is time to start this activity." Because this is a silent and independent activity, students will pass the container quickly and with little noise or disruption, so this can occur while other activities are happening such as announcements.

When it is time to begin the activity, begin by explaining the research finding that groups will consistently make better decisions than the smartest person in the group, as long as (1) the group is sufficiently diverse; (2) each individual in the group has a way to give input independently of the others; and (3) there is an efficient way to aggregate the input. As a quick and easy example of this phenomenon, you can reference the "poll the audience" choice in game shows in which contestants are able to seek help with difficult questions by polling the audience for their knowledge of the topic. Polling the audience provides all three of the conditions just listed, and contestants who used this method during the course of one famous game show received the right answer 91% of the time, compared to the 61% accuracy of phoning a single expert waiting at home.

Ask each person in the group in turn to read aloud their guess of the number of items in the glass container. Stress that students must remain true to their guesses, and *must not* alter their number, regardless of how ridiculous their guess may seem compared to other estimates read aloud before theirs. As each student recites his or her guess, enter the number in a calculator, and when all the numbers are added calculate the mean by dividing the total by the number of individual guesses. In order to be certain your calculation is correct, quickly repeat the process.

Surprisingly, you will find the mean produced by the group's guesses will be closer to the actual number of items in the container than the majority of individual guesses. In many cases the group mean will be closer than all of the individual guesses! Even when an individual guess or two are more accurate than the group-derived mean, research has shown that these individuals will not *consistently* perform even close to the group level of accuracy.

Debriefing Questions   *Time*: 13 minutes

- What does this activity suggest about what makes groups wise?
- What does this activity suggest about the importance of each group member's voice in the decision-making process?
- How might a discussion leader increase the chance in a group discussion that every member is heard from and feels empowered to share their unique perspective?
- Research has shown that brainstorming—when group members speak spontaneously, led and inspired by each other's thoughts—produces much less accurate decision-making results. Why might this be?
- What specific techniques might a leader employ when trying to approximate the conditions necessary to bring out the wisdom of a group? What about situations in which conversation must replace mathematical aggregation?

Activity Variation   The times listed for both of these activities are the minimum recommendations. The Leaderless! exercise can easily accommodate a longer period of instructor silence. With longer periods of silence, such as 45 minutes, the instructor may *very* sparingly offer a process comment or two designed to raise group awareness, such as "I find it interesting that the males in this class have made all the decisions about conversational structure." Such statements must be made dispassionately, with no further elaboration, and the instructor must immediately resume the neutral, unresponsive posture after the statement is made.

❯ Facilitator Notes

For the Leaderless! exercise, it is helpful for the group to understand that time is being kept during this exercise. For instance, I make a show of taking off my watch right before giving the group their instruction and laying it on my desk in front of me. This exercise is adapted from the Tavistock Conference literature (see Molenkamp & Hayden, 2003).

For the research behind the Wisdom of Crowds activity, see Surowiecki (2004).

❯ References

Molenkamp, R. J., & Hayden, C. (2003). *Tavistock primer II*. Unpublished manuscript

Surowiecki, J. (2004). *The wisdom of crowds*. New York: Anchor Books.

Steve Mills is associate director of the Center for Leadership and Social Change at Florida State University. He also teaches *Leadership in Groups and Communities* in the Center's Leadership Certificate program.

Active Learning Module 3e

Being Ethical

David Rosch, Kirstin Phelps

> ## Summary of Concepts

This learning module addresses the "Being Ethical" portion of Chapter 3, The Relational Leadership Model. Practicing ethical leadership requires students to understand how to integrate and apply various related concepts, such as how students' personal values undergird their decision making and how morality and ethical behavior are related in building group relationships.

> ## Learning Outcomes

Students will

- Consider the definitions of the following seven concepts: ethics, integrity, values, morals, character, relationships, and conflict
- Understand what a "concept map" is and how to build one

- Apply the idea of a concept map to the seven concepts just mentioned
- Consider how their concept map can be applied to their own leadership practices

> Module Overview

In this learning module, students learn about "concepts maps" as a way of expressing the relationships between concepts related to the ethical practice of leadership. Specifically, students are introduced to the following concepts and place them in relationship with one another to aid in their practice of ethical leadership:

- Ethics
- Integrity
- Values
- Morals
- Character
- Relationships
- Conflict

After a brief discussion of why effective leadership needs to be ethical leadership, students review the seven concepts, including their definitions. Then students are introduced to the idea of a concept map and in small groups create their own concept maps of these terms.

Estimated Time
Activity 1: Large Group Discussion Connecting Ethics to Leadership, 10 minutes
Activity 2: Introduction of Concepts and Concept Mapping, 20 minutes
Activity 3: Concept Map Creation in Small Groups, 20 minutes
Activity 4: Reflection on Personal Practice Pair and Share, 10 minutes

Materials/Supplies

Flip chart paper or white board with markers

Handouts and/or public display of seven concepts

Sets of seven index cards—one concept written on each
　　card/one set per small group, with the word's definition written
　　on the back

Predetermined reflection sheets, one per student (optional)

> Module Activities

Activity 1: Connecting Ethics to Leadership

Time: 10 minutes

　　Begin the module by mentioning to students that "good" leadership often has two meanings: (1) good, meaning "effective" or successful at reaching the goal and (2) good, meaning "moral." However, the book *Exploring Leadership* implies that for leaders to be effective, they must *also* be moral. Ask the group, "Why do you think the book's authors make that assertion?" Allow some responses from individuals in the group, and make sure to write them publicly.

　　These responses will serve as a backdrop for the remainder of the session. If a student doesn't mention it, make sure to add that today's definition of leadership from *Exploring Leadership* underscores the significance of working with others to create positive change; at the foundation of this change-making is the idea of ethical behavior in relationships.

　　Ask the group, "Is acting ethically easy to do?" Most students are likely to respond, "no." Agree with the group, mentioning that we are often faced with temptations that put pressure on us to act unethically. Make sure to mention that while ethical behavior is sometime difficult to practice, what makes it even more challenging is that sometimes, even deciding on what is ethical is difficult.

Ethical decision making requires:

- Knowledge of one's own values, as well as the values of one's group
- An understanding of what is moral within the context of the situation
- Strength of character
- An ability to build strong relationships
- Competence in navigating conflict

After a short discussion of these items, mention that the remainder of the session is dedicated to exploring how all these things fit together to create an ethically effective leader.

Activity 2: Introduction to Concepts

Time: 20 minutes

Place the students in groups of three to four (large enough to create energy; small enough so that each individual is called to participate). Publicly display the following words:

- Ethics
- Integrity
- Values
- Morals
- Character
- Relationships
- Conflict

Give groups approximately 10 minutes to come up with a definition of each word that each participant finds acceptable. (You might challenge them to do this without use of the Internet!) After 10 minutes, allow a handful of groups to share a few of their definitions.

Distribute handouts (or publicly display slides) that include the following definitions:

- *Ethics*—Principles or standards governing behavior of an individual or organization
- *Integrity*—Acting consistently according to a firmly established character pattern; "doing the right thing"
- *Values*—Core beliefs that guide an individual's thoughts or actions based on the ends he or she desires
- *Morals*—Guidelines arising from one's conscience in discerning good from evil
- *Character*—The overall mark of a person's words and actions, determined from long-term behavior; quality of honesty and courage
- *Relationships*—Emotional connections between people
- *Conflict*—An incompatibility or quarrel between parties, ideas, or goals

Make sure to mention that these definitions are not the *only* definitions that exist for these concepts, but they will be the working definitions used in the remainder of the session. Even if students disagree over them, ask whether they would be willing to adopt these definitions for the time that the group is together.

After reviewing each term, ask the large group to provide an example or two of what this term "looks like." Examples might include

- *Ethics*—A student code of conduct; the Ten Commandments; or ethical standards for the medical profession
- *Integrity*—When someone follows through on their promises
- *Values*—Honesty, family, achievement, or fairness, and so forth.
- *Morals*—How a person decides if he or she is "good" or not

- *Character*—Standing up to bullies; or always being respectful to others even in disagreement
- *Relationships*—Family, romantic, and so forth
- *Conflict*—Disagreements over priorities, resources, and so on.

Once the group is clear on definitions, ask whether students have ever heard of concept maps. Explain that a concept map is simply a visual representation of the relationship between concepts, just as a map in an atlas is a visual representation of relationship between geographic places. Many people use concept maps to help understand or explain how complex concepts interact with one another in practice.

Figure 3.1 is an example of a concept map (that describes a concept map).

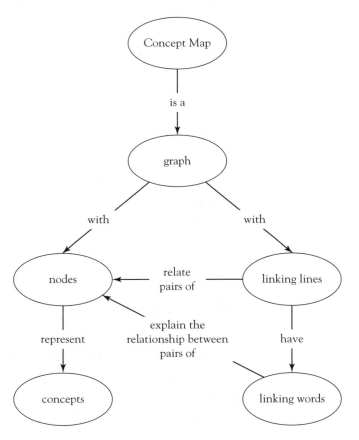

Figure 3.1   **Concept Map**

Facilitators might choose to draw a simple version of this publicly to help students understand. Explain that in the following activity, students will be creating a concept map using the seven terms we just reviewed.

Activity 3: Concept Map Creation

Time: 20 minutes

Place students back in groups of three to four. Note: it might be helpful to have them in the same groups as before, as these groups already worked to create definitions of the seven concepts. Distribute packs of cards that include each of the seven words, with their definition stated on the back. Give each of the small groups 15 minutes to create their own unique concept map of how ethics, integrity, values, morals, character, relationships, and conflict are in tangible relationship with each other to create ethical leadership. During this time, the facilitator should be visiting groups, helping those who are struggling by asking them questions such as

- Is one concept more central to ethical leadership than the others? If so, how?
- Is there a concept that should be "on top" or "on the bottom?"
- Can someone have integrity without ethics and values?
- How do conflict and relationships affect a leader's character?

After 15 minutes, bring attention back to the larger group and ask if any groups would like to share their concept map. Make sure to have them explain why they designed theirs as they did, as their rationale is more important to group learning than their literal placement of concepts. Share with the group that there is no one "correct" concept map that explains in all cases how these concepts interrelate for every person, but that effective leaders often are conscious of their own "personal concept map."

Activity 4: Reflection on Personal Practice

Time: 10 minutes

Either ask students to take out a sheet of paper or distribute a reflection sheet with predetermined questions to respond to. Items the facilitator might want to have students consider:

- What is the most difficult part about leading ethically for you? Why?
- How might you utilize others to help you grow as an ethical leader?

After a few minutes of quiet writing time, ask students to pair up with someone else in the group to discuss their answers. After a few more minutes, use the remaining time available to ask for volunteers to share what they discussed with their partner and to review the concepts that seemed most salient for the group.

> Facilitator Notes

Students may want to discuss how certain famous (or infamous) leaders might be considered "effective" by segments of society while not acting with "good" intentions. This tension is often related to a larger tension around the definition of leadership and what is considered effective in modern society. The goal of this session is not to engage students in a debate on the topic. This also relates to how the other definitions are discussed. If students disagree, invite them to "rent" the definition of leadership used in the session for the time the group is together.

Facilitators may need to be prepared that students may not have heard of concept mapping before, and therefore may need some help to begin their work together. If groups seem to be struggling, ensure that the degree of support they receive from you is more closely aligned with the challenges they are facing.

Dr. David Rosch is an assistant professor in agricultural education at the University of Illinois at Urbana-Champaign, where he teaches leadership courses and studies college student leadership development. He earned his doctorate in higher education administration from Syracuse University.

Kirstin Phelps is a program director in the Illinois Leadership Center at the University of Illinois at Urbana-Champaign. She earned her MS in agricultural education from the University of Illinois.

Active Learning Module 3f

Being Process Oriented

Chris Bohle

> Summary of Concepts

This learning module addresses the "Being Ethical" portion of Chapter 3, The Relational Leadership Model. In the chapter, the authors describe *process* as "how the group goes about being a group, remaining a group, and accomplishing a group's purposes." Student leaders need to learn to be attentive to not only the tasks of the group, but also the processes the group uses as it goes about its work. In highly effective groups, processes are intentional, not happenstance. Leaders give careful consideration to issues such as how members are recruited and welcomed, how ideas are shared, how decisions are made, and how disagreements are addressed. Being process-oriented means that all members of the group are conscious of issues related to process, by being reflective, collaborative, and attending to shared meaning-making.

> Learning Outcomes

Students will

- Be able to articulate their personal definition of terms from the chapter, such as cooperation, collaboration, reflection, and meaning-making

- Develop awareness of process-related issues in a group
- Practice reflection and meaning-making in a structured setting

> Module Overview

Students participate in a problem-solving activity followed by a large group reflective discussion of their process.

Estimated Time:
Activity 1: Self-Facilitated Activity, 30 minutes
Activity 2: Debrief discussion and "Being Reflective," 15 minutes
Activity 3: Being Reflective discussion, 15 minutes

Materials/Supplies
A whiteboard and dry-erase markers (for constructing the group definition)
Video camera
Television/computer
Cord connecting video and audio feed to instructor's viewing room

> Module Activities

Activity 1: Self-Facilitated Activity

Time: 30 minutes

For this activity, the facilitator watches the students' process from another room while they determine how to accomplish the assigned task on their own. While this may seem simple, many students are used to being given structure rather than developing one with each other.

Before the group arrives, set up a video camera with a live feed to a separate computer (or a webcam with a Skype feed to your computer). Prepare instructions such that students will receive them without your presence (either a poster, handout, or PowerPoint presentation already running). These instructions should explain the following:

- Your facilitator is observing your group process from another room via camera feed. This is not being recorded.
- Your task is to discuss the following question: What is the difference between cooperation and collaboration, and do you agree that those approaches are more effective than competition (why or why not)?
- As a group, you should create a performance piece (such as a skit, dance, or musical performance) that conveys your shared understanding of these concepts and their compared effectiveness.
- You will have until [state the time] to complete this challenge.
- Be aware of your "process" for discussion later.

When students are ready to give their presentation, the facilitator should enter the room, turn off the camera, and view the performance.

Debriefing the Activity   *Time*: 15 minutes

Following the performance, bring the students back together in a circle to begin debriefing the experience. The students probably experienced a range of emotions during this open and unguided exercise. Talk about the positive and negative feelings that occurred during the experience. Use the following questions to guide discussion:

Debrief Questions
- What did you think when you came into the room and there were instructions without a facilitator?
- How would you rate the difficulty of this experience on a scale of 1–10 (1 being a breeze and 10 being excruciatingly difficult)?

- What were the difficult parts?
- What did the group struggle with?
- What did the group do well?
- Rather than the content of what was discussed, what did you notice about *how* it was discussed?
  - How did others react initially to this exercise? How did the group get started?
  - How were opinions and ideas shared?
  - How did the group take advantage of the different ways members could contribute? (Did they share what talents they each had to use in the performance?)
  - How were disagreements or differences of opinion handled?
  - What are other aspects of process you observed?
- Were any aspects of the group's process *intentionally* decided, as opposed to just emerging?
  - Students may need you to share your own observations here. Help them come to see certain statements as "being process-oriented." Typical examples are when students say "let's vote to decide" or "let's go around the circle and each share our own opinions."
- Who practiced leadership well?
  - How are you defining "leadership" when you identify those people? Remind the group that in *Exploring Leadership* (3rd edition) leadership is defined as a process all members of the group are engaged in.
  - Did a discussion leader emerge or was this leadership role shared? How did the group come to have that approach?
  - What are some of the other leadership roles they observed people engaging in?
- What does it mean for leaders to "be process-oriented?"

Being Reflective Discussion   *Time:* 15 minutes
  Connect students to the aspects of the chapter related to reflection and contemplation, "Reflection is the process of

pausing, stepping back from the action, and asking, What is happening? Why is this happening? What does this mean? What does this mean for me? What can I learn from this?"

- The instructions described having an awareness of process. What was it like trying to be observant and aware of the process while being simultaneously engaged in the process?
- What is the connection between being reflective and being process-oriented?
- Do you typically have this awareness of process while engaging in other groups?
- Is being reflective of process something that anyone can learn to do?
- What are the barriers to being a reflective leader? How might those be addressed?
- Have you been involved in groups that are reflective of their process together?
  - What might that look like? What are creative ways to engage groups in being collectively reflective about how they go about being a group?

Variations   Rather than a skit, students may be given art supplies, tinker-toys, Legos or other materials to construct an artifact that communicates their shared perspective on the concepts and their compared effectiveness.

In another variation, rather than a video-feed, the activity could be conducted as a fishbowl exercise. A subset of the group sits in the center to do the activity while the rest of the group observes their process and takes notes. Students should be instructed to take notes, not on the content of the discussion but on how the group is approaching the task: Is one person facilitating? Is everyone jumping in? Are they being inclusive of everyone's ideas? Occasionally, the facilitator can tap observers to take the place of a person "in the fishbowl" to give students the experience of both observing and taking part in the process.

> Facilitator Notes

The facilitator should plan out this module *very* deliberately since the instruction during the activity is minimal to nonexistent. Given the lack of instructor presence, try the following steps to ensure a positive experience for participants.

- Sometimes the video camera malfunctions. Have a contingency plan that does *not* involve you coming into the room. The best solutions would be to have someone from an audiovisual department "on call" or to have the phone number of one of the participants should anything go wrong.
- Hang up signs so the students don't think you aren't coming to the session. Make it abundantly clear that your lack of presence is purposeful.
- Put up signs so the participants know where to find you.
- Setup before *any* students arrive. The exercise runs best if no one sees you. Ideally, the class arrives to an empty classroom with a video tape running.
- Share (in writing in the room) that you are watching the live feed but *not* recording content. If you would like to record for the class to debrief at a later date, inform them that recording is happening.
- Take detailed notes of the groups' approach to this task. Referring to specific comments or occurrences will aid in your postactivity discussion.

Chris Bohle is the associate director of Student Life at Hope College in Holland, Michigan. He is a graduate of Loyola University-Chicago and Spring Arbor University and has researched and published work on leadership development and leadership programs. He has also served as a collaborative researcher for the Multi-Institutional Study of Leadership.

Active Learning Module 4a

Exploring Strengths

Katherine Hershey Conlon

> Summary of Concepts

This learning module addresses a portion of Chapter 4, Understanding Yourself. In this section, students learn about the critical role of self-awareness in effective leadership. An important part of self-awareness is developing a deeper understanding of our natural talents and strengths, how to practice and build upon them, and how to use them to achieve our goals. In this pursuit, self-reflection can be one of the best and most essential leadership development tools we have.

It is also important to consider how our individual backgrounds and relationships have influenced the development of particular talent themes in different ways; we may have had more opportunity to practice and develop some talents, whereas some of our talents may be working against us if we are not practicing how to use them effectively.

> Learning Outcomes

Students will

- Reflect on the ways their talents manifest in their daily lives and how these talents can be leveraged to accomplish goals
- Explore and discuss how their top five talents interact with and influence one another and learn about the similarities and differences in the ways talents manifest differently in different people
- Think about nontalents or talents in "overdrive" and identify potential complementary partners in their lives who can help manage these areas.

> Module Overview

Students consider individual reflection questions about their top talents and discuss with a partner the ways in which they have used these talents recently and could leverage them in service of a personal goal. Students then use art supplies to create a visual representation of their top talents in action, which they present in small groups, followed by a large group debrief. Finally, students think about what some of their top talents look like in "overdrive," and how to identify and leverage complimentary partners in their lives to help manage this.

Estimated Time
Activity 1: Understanding Your Talents
- Individual reflection: 5 minutes
- Partner discussions: 10 minutes

Activity 2: Talents in Action
- Individual art activity: 10 minutes
- Small group discussion: 10 minutes
- Large group debrief: 10 minutes

Activity 3: What About Weaknesses?
- Individual reflection: 5 minutes
- Small group discussion: 10 minutes

Materials/Supplies

Art supplies (e.g., markers/crayons, paper, glue, pipe cleaners)

Flip chart paper (with reflection questions prewritten on it)

Have students bring the results of the Clifton Strengths-
    Quest (an individual one-use code is available in the
    back of print editions of *Exploring Leadership*, 3rd edi-
    tion, and in the e-book, or you can purchase a code from
    https://www.gallupstrengthscenter.com/Purchase/)

> Module Activities

Activity 1: Understanding Your Talents

Time: 15 minutes

Explain to students that the first step in developing our talents into true strengths is becoming aware of the ways in which
we are already using them. To continue building our capacity
to use our talents effectively we must practice using them
intentionally.

Invite students to choose one of their top five talents, to
reread the definition of that talent and to spend five minutes
individually making some notes about the four reflection
questions.

Post the flip-chart paper that has the following questions
prewritten on it as a reference for their individual reflection
time:

1. What does this talent mean to you? How would you describe
   this talent to someone else in your own words?
2. When was the last time you used this talent?

3. What is a goal you have for yourself? How can you use this talent to help you reach your goal?
4. What are three ways in which you can practice using this talent in the next week?

Then ask students to pair up and discuss their reflections with one another. Invite them to help one another with questions 3 and 4 if they found they were stuck. If there is extra time after both have shared, invite them to talk about another one of their talents, using the same questions as a guide.

Activity 2: Talents in Action

Time: 30 minutes

Explain that two people with the same talent in their top five could still behave very differently. This is due in part to the different contexts within which people are raised. It is also because each of our top five talents interact with the other four, influencing our behavior in a variety of different ways.

Invite students to consider the ways in which their top five talents interact with one another and to use the art supplies provided to draw or create a visual representation of their "talents in action." Some prompting questions could include

How do your talents interact with one another?
How do these interactions show up in your day-to-day behavior?
Are there times when some talents show up more than others?
What do your talents allow you to do?

Then in groups of two to four, students should share their work. Encourage them to ask one another questions.

Debrief this activity with the large group. Particularly take time to explore the similarities and differences in how talents manifest among people who have some of the same talents.

Activity 3: What About Weaknesses?

Time: 15 minutes

Explain to students that a "weakness" can either be an area of "nontalent" *or* one of our talents "in overdrive." When a talent is in overdrive, it is being used ineffectively and in an extreme way that is not helpful. A few examples:

Empathy in overdrive can lead someone to be perceived as a pushover.

Command in overdrive can lead someone to be perceived as overly bossy.

Futuristic in overdrive can lead someone to be perceived as unrealistic.

Ask students to pick one of their top five talents and to reflect individually on the following questions:

What does this talent look like in overdrive?

How can you leverage your *other* talents to manage this more effectively?

Think of a person in your life who has a different and complimentary talent. How might she or he be able to help you recognize when you are in overdrive?

Allow students to discuss in groups of two to four.

› Facilitator Notes

Students will need to have completed the Clifton StrengthsQuest instrument prior to class. You will either need to require that they bring the description of their top five talents with them to class, or have a reference card with definitions of all 34 Talent Themes available for students to reference. (You can download this reference card from www.strengthsquest.com, under the "Strengths Educators" and "Resources" Tab. The document is called "All 34 Themes Full Description.")

Please keep in mind that it is a matter of ethical practice to not reveal a student's results of this or any assessment to other participants. Students may reveal their own results to the extent they are comfortable, but facilitators should not design activities that release these results publicly.

You may want to investigate whether someone on your campus has been through one of Gallup's Strengths Educator Seminars. If so, inviting this person to help in presenting some of the context and background on a strengths-based approach may be helpful.

Katherine Hershey Conlon, a former leadership and service-learning practitioner and teacher, is currently working as a consultant and coach. She received an MA in counseling and personnel services (college student personnel) from the University of Maryland and is finishing a master of applied positive psychology at the University of Pennsylvania.

Self-Awareness:
Strengths, Values, and Beliefs

Sunshine Workman

> ## Summary of Concepts

This learning module addresses the Identifying Your Passions and Strengths and Values, Beliefs, Ethics, and Character sections of Chapter 4, Understanding Yourself. Self-awareness and self-acceptance are essential ingredients to having presence. People are naturally drawn to those who know who they are and what they are about. Greater self-knowledge yields inspiring relationships built on mutual trust and collaboration. Identifying and articulating one's core values and beliefs in a coherent operating philosophy serves as a compass to help navigate the trials and tribulations associated with being in a leadership role.

> ## Learning Outcomes

Students will

- Be able to identify personal stories that exemplify their talents and strengths
- Be able to articulate five core values

- Apply active-listening techniques that result in greater authenticity
- Be able to create a personal vision or "philosophy" statement that encompasses their strengths, values, and beliefs

> Module Overview

In this module, the facilitator first sets the context of the workshop through a brief, large-group discussion on thoughts about the connection between one's purpose and leadership effectiveness. Following, students engage in personal reflection, identifying five core values and stories from childhood that showcase their Clifton StrengthsQuest themes.

Students are then engaged in a small group active-listening watercolor activity. In groups of three, each student shares his or her story while the other two listen. This is followed by a period of silence in which each person paints impressions of what he or she heard. These paintings are then shared with the storyteller. This cycle repeats until everyone has played the role of speaker. The active-listening watercolor activity tends to break down barriers and adds a dimension of healthy vulnerability, which often results in the speaker feeling comfortable to share more deeply.

The module concludes with a large group discussion on the relationship between self-awareness and leadership effectiveness.

Estimated Time

Activity 1: Personal Visioning, 5-minute large-group list building, 10-minute individual reflection

Activity 2: Sharing Our Stories, 35-minute arts-based listening activity

Activity 3: Connecting Theory to Practice, 10-minute large group debrief

Materials/Supplies

Pan washable watercolors (1–2 per group)

Water container (1 per group)

Thick 4 x 4 watercolor paper (3 per person)

Watercolor brushes (1 per person)

> Module Activities

Activity 1: Personal Visioning Reflection

Time: 15 minutes

Explain to students that this activity is about increasing self-awareness through personal reflection and storytelling. Begin by having the students build a list on the board of the benefits of self-awareness in relationship to leadership effectiveness.

Next, students do a 10-minute individual written reflection, either by responding to the steps as described by you, or by completing the worksheet corresponding to this learning module in the Exploring Leadership Student Workbook.

Step 1: Identify your top five core values   Core values are beliefs about what matters most that serve as broad guidelines for behavior. Write down your top five values, along with your personal definition of each. Additional/optional values identification questions include: (1) Why do you believe this value is important? (2) How do you live into this value? How do you use this value to make decisions? How do you know that you are living into this value?

Step 2: Identify strengths from stories in the past   Thinking back to childhood is a good way to identify early signs of Clifton StrengthsQuest themes because, for most of us, this was when we spent the most time playing. Reflecting on the following questions, what are 1–3 stories that showcase your signature strength themes?

- What did you love to do?
- What activities caused you to lose track of time?
- What kinds of things did people ask for your help with?
- Where did you feel a sense of mastery or curiosity?

Step 3: Personal vision statement Have students imagine that it is five years from now. Ask, "What do you want to be able to say about your life?" Helpful reflection questions include: What do you see as the connection between the themes of your signature strengths and core values? What future do you want to be able to say you lived into? What do you want your friends to say about you? Your coworkers? Your community? Those who are marginalized? Your life partner?

In a simple phrase, write a powerful statement that describes what you want to be. There is not really a "right" way to do this other than it feels right to you. When you look at it, does your body tingle? Do you feel excited and full of joy when you read it? Does it pull you forward?

Activity 2: Sharing Our Stories

Time: 35 minutes

Provide a brief overview of the activity with explicit instructions on the activity. The basic format of this activity is four minutes of individual storytelling, two minutes painting in silence, and two minutes of small group sharing. Then the cycle repeats until everyone in the group has gone.

Instructions
- Each person will have four minutes to share thoughts on the following questions:
  - What was one value that stood out to you?

- What is one story from the past that exemplifies a top strength?
- Then there will be two minutes of painting in silence. Paint the words or images that stood out to you the most. These "paintings" are quick impressions. Don't worry about whether or not you are a "good artist." You can keep it abstract if you wish. The speaker can feel free to rest and relax while others paint or to paint the images that came to mind during the storytelling.
- Group members will then have four minutes to share the pictures, along with what stood out to them about the speaker's story. At the end, give the storyteller your painting.

Tips on active listening to share with students:

- Rather than asking questions and thinking of what to say next, this activity focuses on the fine art of listening.
- Give your full attention to the speaker and listen so that they share more deeply.
- Be aware that encouraging or discouraging nonverbal messages can change the nature of what is shared. Focus on being an open and reflective mirror.
- Only one person has the microphone at a time. The full sharing time is his or her time to use. If the person has nothing more to share, sit in silence until the allotted time ends.
- Be mindful of airtime in the group sharing process so that everyone has a chance to speak.

Activity 3: Connecting Theory to Practice

Time: 10 minutes

As a large group, debrief the activity and connect the experience to the relationship between self-awareness and leadership effectiveness.

Debriefing Questions

- What was it like to speak?
- What was it like to listen?
- How does active listening change your relationship with others?
- How were your values similar or different?
- What did you notice about vulnerability, authenticity, and building relationships?

› Facilitator Notes

Let students know that this is a "challenge by choice" activity. They can go as deep or on the surface as feels safe to them but are encouraged to stretch themselves.

Sunshine Workman is the Immersion Experiences program manager in the Cal Corps Public Service Center at the University of California, Berkeley. Sunshine currently supports the Shinnyo-en Peacebuilding Leadership Program, the W.T. Chan Fellowship program, and the Alternative Breaks program.

Active Learning Module 4c

Leadership Skills Assessment

William Smedick

> **Summary of Concepts**

This learning module addresses Chapter 4, Understanding Yourself. In this chapter, students learn about the importance of self-awareness and facilitating one's own growth as a leader, referred to as self-leadership development. An important aspect of understanding the self and self-leadership development involves taking time to be reflective about one's strengths and skills. Self-assessment exercises are an excellent way to facilitate that self-awareness and self-leadership development. As noted in Chapter 4, Bennis's (1989) described four lessons for developing self-knowledge:

- You are your own best teacher.
- Accept responsibility. Blame no one.
- You can learn anything you want to learn.
- True understanding comes from reflection on your experience. (p. 56)

Because attempting to accomplish positive change is foundational to the definition of leadership in *Exploring Leadership* (3rd edition), this module focuses on a self-assessment of the leadership skills that are connected to facilitating change.

> Learning Outcomes

Students will

- Understand the concept of self-leadership development
- Be able to identify the essential skills associated with successfully leading change
- Be able to identify their competency regarding each skill
- Develop a plan to increase competency for at least one skill

> Module Overview

In this exercise, students are presented a list of the essential skills needed to facilitate change in themselves and in organizations. Working in dyads, students self-assess their level of competence on each of these skills. Finally, students explore the concept of leadership self-development and create a development plan for a selected skill.

Estimated Time
Activity 1: Introduce Concepts, 10 minutes
Activity 2: Self-Assessment Procedure, 35 minutes
Activity 3: Development Plan, 10 minutes

Materials and Supplies
Leading Change Leadership Skills Self-Assessment handout for
     each participant.
Writing implement for each participant

> Module Activities

Activity 1: Introduce Concepts

Time: 10 minutes

Begin with a facilitated discussion about the section of Chapter 4 related to self-leadership development, particularly highlighting Bennis's (1989) four lessons for developing self-knowledge:

- You are your own best teacher.
- Accept responsibility. Blame no one.
- You can learn anything you want to learn.
- True understanding comes from reflection on your experience. (p. 56)

Ask students to share examples of when they were able to turn experience into a leadership lesson. After gathering several examples, highlight the role of reflection and self-awareness in those examples. Introduce the following self-assessment activity as another approach to self-awareness and self-leadership development.

Activity 2: Self-Assessment Procedure

Time: 35 minutes

Have students pair into dyads and allow time for a few minutes of introduction. If you are using the Exploring Leadership Student Workbook, have students refer to the skills self-assessment that corresponds with this learning module. Otherwise, you can walk the students through the items verbally, having them mark their responses on their own sheet of paper.

Working section by section, explain the competency in each section, as well as the dimensions described. Have students reflect individually on their own skill level and write down their own perceived level of competency.

Then, in dyads, one student should explain his or her rating and justify it with the examples that came to mind as each dimension was considered. Partners should be instructed to be active listeners, asking clarifying questions and helping their partner have a considered self-assessment. Partners then switch roles. When both partners have shared, the facilitator can then move the group on to the next competency section.

The following are the items in the skills self-assessment. For each item, students should write down the rating that best represents their self-perceived current skill level for each item. You might write the following scale on the board to help clarify:

6 = I feel I am fully competent with nothing left to develop and, if called upon, I can effectively teach others

5 = very competent and that others' learning increases as a result of working with me

4 = personal competence and that I can use this skill in various situations effectively

3 = somewhat competent where I am applying and practicing and I am improving as I gain more experience

2 = I recognize the skill as essential and I am purposefully gaining the knowledge and information to understand

1 = beginning to gain the knowledge

(*Source*: Allen, Julian, Stern, & Walborn, 1987)

Self Development   Developing perspectives, insight, and understanding about ourselves is something we are often too busy to do. We may not even know how to go about doing it. This program provides structure and ideas to help you develop skills related to getting the most out of yourself.

Self-development has two main dimensions: *self-awareness* and *self-management*.

Developing *self-awareness* involves assessing your own strengths, weaknesses, values, motivations, passions, and your own leadership style. It helps you verbalize and prioritize what is important to you.

Have students self-rate on the scale of 1–6, their assessment of their own skill level and knowledge pertaining to self-awareness.

Developing *self-management* skills involves learning about your own sense of integrity, initiative, accountability, adaptability, goal setting, and wellness. It teaches you to stop and reflect on how you view things.

Have students self-rate on the scale of 1–6, their assessment of their own skill level and knowledge pertaining to self-management is.

Pause for students to discuss their ratings in dyads.

Interpersonal Development   Interpersonal skills are always high on the list of characteristics that employers and organizations look for in people. They are skills that will help you build better relationships with everyone you interact with at work, at home, and in your community.

Developing *communication skills* is about learning how to listen. It is about effectively communicating within cultures and between cultures in nonverbal, verbal, and written formats.

Have students self-rate on the scale of 1–6, their assessment of their own skill level and knowledge pertaining to communication skills.

Developing *ethical practices* will build your awareness and ability to empower people and use your own power in positive ways. It will improve your decision making and help you exert influence in synergistic ways, as well as teach you the importance of integrity in fostering and maintaining interpersonal relationships.

Have students self-rate on the scale of 1–6, their assessment of their own skill level and knowledge pertaining to ethical practices.

Team development emphasizes building critical skills for use in team environments such as facilitation, collaboration, conflict resolution, followership, compromise, and assessing group dynamics.

Have students self-rate on the scale of 1–6, their assessment of their own skill level and knowledge pertaining to team development.

Pause for students to discuss their ratings in dyads.

Organizational and Group Development　Organizational and group development has four main dimensions: leading change, project and program effectiveness, system thinking, and community building.

Developing skills in *leading change* is critical to your future as well as the future of others. We live in a dynamic world that demands skills such as visioning, creativity, risk-taking, personal resiliency, and modeling in everything we do. We all recognize the value of leading change rather than being left behind.

Have students self-rate on the scale of 1–6, their assessment of their own skill level and knowledge pertaining to leading change.

Developing skills in *project and program effectiveness* are vital to the success of any organization. We can help you develop your ability to organize, budget, plan, delegate, and continuously improve. Because organizations are made up of people, it is important to recognize accomplishment, celebrate success, retain valuable human assets, document progress, and assess the impact of variables that affect your organization.

Have students self-rate on the scale of 1–6, their assessment of their own skill level and knowledge pertaining to project and program effectiveness.

Developing *systems thinking* skills can enhance your ability to analyze the complexity of organizational environments. It can also help you develop perspectives in critical thinking and build competencies in assessing the effect of environmental factors on your organization. It can help you understand how politics play a part in organizational contexts and even show you how to use technology.

Have students self-rate on the scale of 1–6, their assessment of their own skill level and knowledge pertaining to systems thinking.

Developing *community building* skills is inherent to any organization, because every organization is a community of people. Hopkins Leadership can help you learn more about citizenship, cultural understanding, and coalition building.

Have students self-rate on the scale of 1–6, their assessment of their own skill level and knowledge pertaining to community building.

Pause for students to discuss their ratings in dyads.

Transitional Development   Transitions happen continuously throughout our lives. Graduating from college. Getting a job. Building a career. Getting involved in clubs, organizations, and civic groups. Discovering new places, people, and ideas. Transitions you plan for and stuff that just happens unexpectedly.

Transitional leadership helps you make the most out of your transitions. It will also help you contribute in the best way possible to your family, coworkers, employees, friends, and people you have never even met.

Transitional leadership has only one dimension. It is an important one: *sustaining leadership*. Developing sustaining leadership skills will help you realize your goals. More important, it will help others reach their goals.

Sustaining leadership is about networking with others and making sure that perpetual learning is available to all of us. It is about coaching, developing others, and mentoring. It is about sharing experiences, knowledge, and insight.

Have students self-rate on the scale of 1–6, their assessment of their own skill level and knowledge pertaining to sustaining leadership.

Pause for students to discuss their ratings in dyads.

Activity 3: Development Plan

Time: 10 minutes

At the conclusion, have students pick one dimension on which they would like to increase their competency and develop a plan to do so. Student should first share their plans in their dyads, then share with a full group discussion on the plans and their concluding thoughts on the role of self-awareness and self-initiated development in the ongoing process of learning to be a leader.

> References

University of Illinois Champaign/ Urbana, Leadership Center (Ignite Program).

Allen, K., & Cherry, C. (2000). *Systemic leadership: Enriching the meaning of our work.* American College Personnel Association and National Association for Campus Activities.

Allen, K. E., & Cherrey, C. (2000). *Systemic leadership: Enriching the meaning of our work.* Lanham, MD: University Press of America.

Allen, K., Julian, F., Stern, C., & Walborn, N. (1987). *Future perfect: A guide for professional development and competence.* Columbia, SC: National Association for Campus Activities Educational Foundation.

Bennis, W. G. (1989). *On becoming a leader.* Reading, MA: Addison-Wesley.

William Smedick is the director of Leadership Programs and Assessment in the Office of Student Life at Johns Hopkins University. He is also a lecturer in the Center for Leadership Education in the Hopkins School of Engineering.

Active Learning Module 5a

Developing a Multicultural Mindset

Mark Anthony Torrez

◇

> Summary of Concepts

This learning module addresses a portion of Chapter 5, Understanding Others. In this section, students explore the process of developing a multicultural mindset in order to effectively lead across differences.

It is essential that students engage in individual awareness-building around personal identity as a prerequisite to better understanding the identities and background experiences of others. Through the reflective process of identifying the "self," the "other," and the commonalities and differences that exist between the two, students enhance their ability to enact a multicultural mindset and engage in perspective-taking, the ability to examine situations or ideas through alternate perceptions of reality.

> Learning Outcomes

Students will

- Be able to articulate the concept of "the single story"
- Identify multiple facets of social identity
- Engage in sensitive dialogue around personal experiences

> Module Overview

Students view the TED Talk "The Danger of a Single Story" and utilize the key concept as a framework for discussing social identity. Activities and dialogue that follow the video clip engage students in the process of identifying multiple facets of their social identities and exploring the connections and conflicts between various aspects of identity. The module ends with guiding questions that enable students to recognize the importance of engaging across difference through a lens of intersectionality.

Estimated Time
Activity 1: The Danger of a Single Story
- Introduction: 2–5 minutes
- View video clip: 20 minutes
- Debrief: 5–8 minutes

Activity 2: Understanding the Complexity of Identity
- Complete worksheet: 10 minutes
- Paired Sharing: 10 minutes
- Group Reflection: 10 minutes

Materials/Supplies
Technology to project online video clip
"The Danger of the Single Story" video clip. This is a TED talk by Chimamanda Adichie. It is available on the TED Talks website (www.ted.com) under the title, "Chimamanda Adichie: The danger of a single story."

Identity Inventory worksheet in the Exploring Leadership Workbook (if using)
Writing utensils

› Module Activities

Activity 1: The Danger of a Single Story

Time: 30 minutes

Begin the activity by revisiting key concepts from the beginning of Chapter 5:

> *Learning from people who are different from you—and recognizing your commonalities—is an important part of your education and essential preparation for the world you will join (Michigan State University, p. 2).*

Explain to the students that they are about to watch a TED Talk video clip that will serve as a framework for the rest of the activity. It may be helpful to provide some background on Chimamanda Adichie for context (provided on the site of this Ted Talk).

Play "The Danger of a Single Story" TED Talk video clip, approximately 20 minutes in length.

Debriefing Questions
- What parts of Chimamanda Adichie's story or talk resonated with you most?
- What is the concept of "The Single Story?" What are the dangers associated with this?
- How does "The Single Story" concept connect to our understanding of identity?

Activity Variation   Depending on the group's level of engagement with dialogue, the first two to three minutes of the video clip may be shown—instead of the entire video clip—to provide additional time for discussion/reflection prior to, or following, the video.

Activity 2: Understanding the Complexity of Identity

Time: 30 minutes

Start with 10 minutes of individual written reflection time. Be sure students are aware that they will be asked to share some of these thoughts with others.

If you are using the Exploring Leadership Student Workbook, direct students to the Identity Reflection Worksheet that corresponds with this learning module. Otherwise, instruct students to describe the parts of their social identity related to:

- Ability
- Gender
- Nationality
- Race/ethnicity
- Religious affiliation
- Sexual orientation
- Socioeconomic status/Class

Then have students continue their written reflections on one or more of the following questions:

- Which of my identities do I think about most frequently? Why might that be? What do I generally think about when it's on my mind?
- Describe a situation in which one or more of your facets of social identity influenced your behavior in the situation or reaction to the situation.
- Describe one or more facets of your social identity in which you feel misunderstood or stereotyped. (Think about the concept of "The Single Story.")

Group students into pairs or triads for personal sharing. Each student should take approximately two to three minutes to share her or his reflections. While one student is sharing, the other(s) in each pair or triad should be actively listening.

After each member of the small groups has shared, bring the students back into a large group for a final debrief.

Debriefing Questions
- What was it like for you to disclose such personal information? For those who found it difficult, why was it difficult?
- What did you learn about your peers that will enhance your working or personal relationships moving forward?
- How does this exercise connect to the reading in Chapter 5?
  - The facilitator should specifically reference the three critical questions from the beginning of the chapter:
    - How am I like no one else here?
    - How am I like some others here?
    - How am I like everyone here?
- What did you learn from this exercise and the video clip "The Single Story" that will assist you in better understanding others and working across difference?

> Facilitator Notes

First and foremost, it is critical to ensure that the group is comfortable sharing personal and sometimes sensitive information. Prior to engaging in emotionally risky exercises, ensure that expectations for behavior have been set (e.g., openness and authenticity, respectful communication, confidentiality).

It is also important to recognize varying levels of identity development within the group. For some students, it may be easy to identify and access facets of their identity. With others, you, as a facilitator, may be needed to prompt deepened introspection or utilize probing questions to help students better recognize and articulate identity.

Mark Anthony Torrez is the assistant director for community engagement within the Office of Student Leadership & Service at Emory University in Atlanta, Georgia. He received his MEd, in college student affairs administration from the University of Georgia and a BA in strategic communication from The Ohio State University.

Active Learning Module 5b

Gender Influences on Leadership

Paige Haber-Curran

> ## Summary of Concepts

This learning module addresses a portion of Chapter 5, Understanding Others. In this section, students learn about gender differences with a particular emphasis on the social construction of gender in society. Gender roles have historically enforced traditional notions of how one should behave. From a young age, people are socialized to act in accordance with these expected gender roles. For boys and men, this means that they are expected to be masculine or be "tough" whereas girls and women are expected to be feminine or "nurturing." Many facets of society reinforce these gender roles, such as family, culture, and media. These gender roles often limit both men and women.

Gender roles also influence the way men and women feel they need to lead. Likewise, gender roles influence people's expectations of how people should lead, expecting men to be more decisive, in charge, and competitive, and expecting women to be more nurturing and relationship-oriented. Continuing to promote gender role expectations in relation to leadership limits the individual leaders and the communities in which they lead. While these expectations and stereotypes do exist, there is a great deal of overlap between the sexes that is worth noting, and both men and women are capable of effective leadership.

> Learning Outcomes

Students will

- Understand that gender roles are socially constructed and reinforced through many facets of society
- Consider how gender roles limit both men and women in leadership
- Discern the value of masculine and feminine approaches to leadership

> Module Overview

Students observe a silent cultural demonstration with one man and one woman (two volunteers are needed). The cultural demonstration focuses on the interaction between the man and the woman that is perceived to be very sexist and patriarchal. The subsequent discussion allows students to focus on perception and socialization as it relates to gender in society.

Then, students engage in a written brainstorming activity in which they identify words that come to mind of how we are socialized to think about men and women in society. As a large group the students identify how these gender roles and stereotypes influence society's perceptions and expectations of men and women as leaders. The group generates a list of attitudes, behaviors, and skills associated with female leaders and male leaders.

In small groups students are given questions to discuss the list that was generated of attitudes, behaviors, and skills of female and male leaders. The discussion focuses on examples that confirm or disconfirm these attitudes, behaviors, and skills from their own experience and identifying which of those attitudes, behaviors, and skills they believe contribute to effective leadership. Each group then shares two or three key parts of their discussion with the large group.

To close, the facilitator shows a short video clip and emphasizes that there is value to both masculine and feminine ways of leading. Further, the facilitator brings up the concept of androgynous leadership, the importance of embracing many approaches to leadership, and how gender roles and stereotypes limit both individuals and communities.

Estimated Time

Activity 1: Cultural Demonstration and Discussion, 10 minutes

Activity 2: Gender Roles in Society, 25 minutes

- Silent written brainstorm: 5 minutes
- Discussion of themes from brainstorm: 10 minutes
- Video clip on gender role stereotypes and brief discussion: 5–10 minutes (depending on clip)

Activity 3: Gender Roles and Leadership Small Group Discussion, 20 minutes

Concluding Remarks and Video Clip, 5 minutes

Materials/Supplies

A pitcher with water in it or a water bottle, two cups, and crackers or cookies for the cultural demonstration

Two chairs for the cultural demonstration

Sticky notes in two colors (e.g., blue and pink)—enough for three per student per color

Board or flip charts with markers to write down points emerging from discussion

Technology to project online video clips (including audio)

A video clip of gender norms and stereotypes portrayed in the
media

Two examples:

"Portrayal of Masculinity and Femininity in the Media
(Michael Duong) [reup]" available on YouTube (8 minutes)

"Portrayal of Gender in Modern Commercials MACS 221
Remix" available on YouTube (3 minutes)

Video clip that shows how society assigns different behaviors to
men and women, yet these assigned behaviors are socially constructed rather than inherently true. This video titled, "Gender Construction 101" is available on YouTube (1.5 minutes).

> Module Activities

Activity 1: Cultural Demonstration

Time: 10 minutes

Setup: Put two tables at the front of the room that are facing
each other and are approximately two feet apart. On a chair or
table nearby set up a pitcher with water in it (or a water bottle),
two cups, and some crackers or cookies.

Identify two volunteers, one male and one female. If possible
bring in two volunteers who are not part of the group; if needed,
choose the volunteers from the group. Brief the volunteers with
these instructions:

*This is a silent demonstration. The two volunteers enter the room. The
man enters first, and the woman follows approximately 10 feet behind. The
man sits down on one of the chairs and puts his feet up on the other chair
in front of him. After the man is seated the woman kneels down on the
floor near the chairs.*

*After five seconds the woman silently stands up and walks over to the
water. She pours water into the two cups and takes the two cups back to
where the man is sitting. She hands one cup to the man, who takes a sip.*

After taking a sip the man turns to the woman and nods to her, signaling that is OK for her to also drink the water. The woman then kneels down near the man and takes a few sips of the water.

After another five seconds the woman silently stands up and walks over to the crackers (or cookies). She brings the crackers back to where the man is sitting and hands the man a cracker. The man takes a small bite of the cracker and then nods to the woman, signaling that it is OK for her to also eat the cracker. The woman then kneels down near the man and takes a few bites of a cracker.[1]

After the demonstration, thank the volunteers, but ask them to stay seated where they are. Ask the students: *What adjectives come to mind when you think about the culture depicted in the demonstration?*

After the participants share the different adjectives, read the following description of the culture out loud to the group:

The culture you just observe worships the earth. Women are the leaders in this society and have complete control. Men's sole purpose is to serve the women. Because of men's inferior role to women, men are not allowed to directly touch the earth. If they walk on the ground, they must immediately raise their feet up off the ground when they get to their destination. Women, on the other hand, are allowed to sit on the ground and touch the earth. The culture you observed is also violent and dangerous. Thus, men must always walk in front of women so they are the first to face harm and so they can protect the women from danger. Additionally, there is a risk that food and drinks may be poisoned. Thus, the men must taste all food and drink before women and must sacrifice themselves to prevent women from being poisoned.

Ask the following question to generate dialogue about the demonstration:

- Why did we initially view this culture as [sexist] and [patriarchal]? (include key adjectives that were present in the initial discussion)

---

[1] Note: This activity is based on of the Albatross Activity and is adapted with permission from the LeaderShape Institute.

- Perception based on our experiences in our society
- Our worldview suggests that someone "serving" someone else is subservient to that person
- The society we live in often privileges men
- In what ways are we socialized throughout our lives to have certain expectations based on gender?
  - Messages growing up from parents, teachers, the media, and in politics; the greater number of men in positions of power

Emphasize the prevalence of gender roles in society. Gender roles are socially constructed expectations of people relating to masculinity and femininity. For something to be socially constructed it means that it is not a hard fact, but rather it a phenomenon that is subjective and has come to be understood as truth through how people see situations, interpret them, and act on them. When you are holding a pencil and you let it go, you know that due to the laws of physics the pencil will drop to the ground. There is not this same truth in gender norms; rather, society has come to make assumptions and false truths about gender.

Activity 2: Gender Roles in Society

Time: 25 minutes

Pass out sticky notes to students. If there are fewer than 20 students pass out a total of six sticky notes to each student (three per color). If there are 20 or more students pass out a total of four sticky notes to each student (two per color). Instruct the students that on three (or two if there are 20+ students) of the sticky notes in a certain color (of your choosing) they should put a word or short phrase depicting a gender norm or stereotype for women in our society (for a total of two or three words or phrases, depending on whether they have two or three sticky notes). On the other three (or two) sticky notes, in the other color, they should put a word or short phrase depicting a gender norm or stereotype for men in our society.

On a chalkboard, whiteboard, or flip chart paper label one side "women are . . ." and one side "men are . . ." Once students complete their six (or four) sticky notes have them put the sticky notes up on the board or flip chart paper under the two categories. Ask four volunteers (two per side of the board) to organize the sticky notes into categories or themes. For example, sticky notes with words such as "nice," "kind," and "friendly" may be grouped together. While the volunteers are organizing the sticky notes into themes ask the remaining students to pair up with someone sitting next to them and to share an example of a gender norm that they have seen or heard most recently about men or women.

Once the volunteers are done organizing the sticky notes ask them to share their "findings" back to the rest of the group on what key themes, patterns, or words emerged. The volunteers should not share all of the words but rather note the patterns or any interesting outliers. Once they have shared the themes ask them to sit back down.

After the volunteers report out ask the group:

- What are your reactions to these themes?
- What themes or words surprise you?
- Where have you heard or seen some of these gender roles and stereotypes depicted or reinforced in society? (For example: in media, families, teachers, church)

Play a video clip on gender norms and stereotypes in the media.

Two examples:
"Portrayal of Masculinity and Femininity in the Media (Michael Duong) [reup]" available on YouTube (8 minutes)
"Portrayal of Gender in Modern Commercials MACS 221 Remix" available on YouTube (3 minutes)

Following the video clip ask the students:

What is problematic about these gender roles and stereotypes? (They are limiting to both women and men. Men and women are capable of doing the same things and having the same interests, they create expectations of how women and men should behave and where they should be taken seriously)

Activity 3: Gender Roles and Leadership

Time: 20 minutes

On the board or flip chart paper write on one side "female leaders should . . . " and "male leaders should . . . " Ask the students: Given the gender norms and stereotypes that were generated in the sticky note activity, what are some attitudes, behaviors, or skills that you feel are expected for male and female leaders? Record the responses on the board or flip chart paper.

Once there is a generous list of attitudes, behaviors, and skills generated, break the students into groups of approximately three to four. In their groups students should spend approximately 10 minutes discussing these three questions:

- What examples do you have of men or women who confirm or disconfirm the attitudes, behaviors, and skills we generated?
- Are there any of these attitudes, behaviors, or skills that are strictly gendered, meaning only men or only women are capable of possessing them?
- Which of these attitudes, behaviors, and skills do you believe contribute to effective leadership?

After the small group discussion ask groups to share two to three key points from their discussion to the large group.

Concluding Remarks (5 minutes)   Show this short video clip "Gender Construction 101," which is available on YouTube. (1:29; Note there is no sound for this video clip).

Conclude by sharing that although gender norms and stereotypes suggest that certain leadership behaviors are gendered, men and women are both capable of leading in a variety of different ways. Expecting certain attitudes, behaviors, and skills of someone based on their gender limits not only that individual but also the organization and community in which he or she is leading.

Dr. Alice Eagly and Dr. Linda Carli are social psychologists who study gender and leadership. Their research suggests that effective leaders demonstrate androgynous leadership behaviors, which are leadership behaviors that incorporate both feminine and masculine ways of leading. Effective leaders are capable of being both communal (or collaborative), which is more of a feminine leadership quality, and "agentic" (or assertive), which is more of a masculine leadership quality. Encourage students to reflect on their own leadership style within this framework of being both communal and assertive.

> Facilitator Notes

Be prepared for a wide range of ideas, thoughts, and emotions to be generated in this session. Some students may have never thought about gender much before, and others may think it about it often. There may be emotions that come about from the activities and discussions that you may want to be aware of and for which you may need to provide follow-up with students individually. Also, be aware of gender dynamics that may be emerging within the group. For example, women participating in the discussion may affirm others or buffer their comments (i.e., "It may just be me, but . . . ") or men may challenge others directly or dominate the conversation. It may be interesting to point out these dynamics to the class as a real life case study.

> References

Eagly, A. H., & Carli, L. L. (2007). *Through the labyrinth: The truth about how women become leaders.* Boston, MA: Harvard Business School Press.

Paige Haber-Curran is assistant professor and program coordinator for the Student Affairs in Higher Education Program at Texas State University-San Marcos. Paige received her PhD in leadership studies from the University of San Diego and her MA in college student personnel from the University of Maryland. Her research focuses on college student leadership development, gender and leadership, leadership programs, and student learning.

Active Learning Module 5c

Cultural Influences on Leadership

Stephanie H. Chang

◇

› Summary of Concepts

This learning module addresses a portion of Chapter 5, Understanding Others. In this section, students explore what culture is and how culture influences their skills in communication, conflict, decision making, and relationship building with others. Culture is a broad term that involves a group's shared thoughts, feelings, symbols, and behaviors. There are multiple ways culture informs and shapes students' assumptions about themselves and others.

Leadership is, in part, navigating and understanding the diversity of groups, organizations, and cultures. Exploring characteristics such as gender, ethnicity, and culture enhances students' intrapersonal and interpersonal leadership capacities.

› Learning Outcomes

Students will

- Deepen their awareness of cultural assumptions held about others

- Consider the importance of strengthening and enhancing cultural knowledge
- Identify how cultural influences are relevant to leadership skills and knowledge

> Module Overview

Students engage in a dyad-dialogue activity where they work toward acknowledging and suspending their assumptions about another person. Through this activity students explore how their assumptions, judgments, or stereotypes of others limits their understanding of others.

Estimated Time
Activity 1: Dyad Dialogue and Reflective Discussion, 30 minutes
Activity 2: Gallery Walk and Small Group Discussion,
   30 minutes

Materials/Supplies
Paper and pens, pencils, markers, or crayons for students
Flip chart paper, markers and tape for the facilitator

> Module Activities

Activity 1: Dyad Dialogues

Time: 30 minutes

    Share with students that this activity is about getting to know themselves through getting to know others. Divide students into pairs or dyads to prepare for their dialogues. Ask students to partner with someone they know less well than others.

    Ask students to identify one person as Person A and the other as Person B. The format of the dyad dialogues is that each pair will take turns sharing background information about themselves such as where they grew up, how many siblings they have, how did or does their family celebrate holidays, or how did their family take vacations. Let students know that during each turn only one person speaks at a time and the other person is actively listening but also tuning into what assumptions they have about their partner's story.

Here is a suggested format of the dyads (20 minutes):

Round One, Part 1: 5 minutes

- Person A Shares: 2 minutes
    - Person A shares/talks about his or her identities or cultures and responds to "who are you" type of prompts
    - Person B listens without any verbal response
- Reflective Writing: 3 minutes
    - Person A, write about what it was like sharing (what did you decide to share or not share and what thoughts did you have while sharing information about yourself to someone else)
    - Person B, write down any assumptions and thoughts you had from listening to Person A and what, if any, questions came up

Round One, Part 2: 5 minutes

- Person B Reveals: 2 minutes
    - Person B shares what he or she wrote about during the previous reflective writing session
    - Person A listens without any verbal response
- Reflective Writing: 3 minutes
    - Person A, write about your assumptions and thoughts from hearing what Person B shared
    - Person B, write about your experience sharing your assumptions and thoughts with and about Person A

Round Two, Part 1: 5 minutes
- Person B Shares: 2 minutes
  - Person A shares/talks about his or her identities or cultures and responds to "who are you" type of prompts
  - Person B listens without any verbal response
- Reflective Writing: 3 minutes
  - Person B, write about what it was like sharing (what did you decide to share or not share and what thoughts did you have while sharing information about yourself to someone else)
  - Person A, write down any assumptions and thoughts you had from listening to Person B and what, if any, questions came up

Round Two, Part 2: 5 minutes
- Person A Reveals: 2 minutes
  - Person A shares what they wrote about during his or her previous reflective writing session
  - Person B, listens without any verbal response
- Reflective Writing: 3 minutes
  - Person B, write about your assumptions and thoughts from hearing what Person A shared
  - Person A, write about your experience sharing your assumptions and thoughts with and about Person B

Debrief Questions and Reflections (15 minutes)   Consider the following questions for debriefing the dyad activity:

- How do you feel?
- What did you learn about someone else?
- What did you learn about yourself?
- What was difficult for you in this activity?
- What assumptions did you make about your dyad partner?

- Why is it relevant to acknowledge the assumptions we carry about others?
- Why is it necessary to recognize how we make assumptions and stereotypes about others?
- How do you compare your background and story with that of your partner?
- What differences or similarities and differences did you notice between you and your partner?
- How did this activity relate to cultural influences in leadership?

Activity Variation　　You can prompt students to respond to specific questions or statements for the first two minutes of each round. For instance, students can share information on their social identities, past vacations with family, religious or spiritual celebrations, or stories about their favorite pastime. The content and types of stories students are asked to share can range from high-risk (more vulnerable narratives) to low-risk (least vulnerable narratives). In either case, the students' stories or information about themselves will carry assumptions, stereotypes, and conclusions made by others.

Activity 2: Gallery Walk

Time: 30 minutes

Share with students that this activity is about exploring our individual and collective backgrounds and how it relates to leadership. Students will have an opportunity to illustrate in images and/or writing a description of their family, typical family vacations, or an important memory from childhood that represents their background. After illustrating their personal and/or family background, students will post their images around the room. Each student will walk around the room and explore the illustrations by noting their thoughts and assumptions about what the illustration communicates.

Here is a suggested order of prompting students into the Gallery Walk:

Give students approximately five to ten minutes to create an illustration that symbolizes their background. If necessary, give students examples such as family traditions, vacations, celebrations, or memories. After completing their illustrations, ask students to post their illustrations around the room. Make sure to ask students *not to include* their names on their illustrations.

Give students approximately 10 minutes to walk around the room silently to observe each illustration. Provide students with an observation guide such as

- What symbols do you see?
- What reactions do you have?
- What assumptions do you make?
- What does this illustration tell you about the individual who made it?

After the first gallery walk, divide students into groups of three to four people. Ask each group to identify as least one illustration to discuss, as a group. Make sure the student who created the illustration is not in the small group reacting to their illustration. Give students at least five to 10 minutes to react to the illustration in their small groups. Ask students to compare

- The differences in their reactions to the illustration
- The similarities in their reactions to the illustration
- Their overall assumptions about the person who drew the illustration

Reconvening in a large group, ask students to share their illustrations. Ask students to share the story behind their illustration and what messages they hoped to convey about their story and background. Depending on time and the size of the group, this portion of the activity may take anywhere from 10 to 30 minutes. So you may want to ask only a few students to share their illustrations.

Debrief Questions and Reflections (10 minutes)   After a few students have shared their illustrations, ask students to respond to the following questions:

- Was this activity uncomfortable for you?
- What was uncomfortable about this activity?
- In general, what type of assumptions did you make about the illustrations?
- How certain were you about your observations?
- What new perspectives came from processing one illustration in a small group from when you made your own individual observation?
- How did this activity relate to cultural influences in leadership?

Make sure to ask students to speak in generalities or avoid identifying specific illustrations to use as an examples.

Activity Variation   There are multiple ways to vary this activity. One is to ask students in small groups to create an illustration that embodies or symbolizes the individuals within their group. Another is to identify images of people from magazines or the Internet that cover a broad range of social identities. If using images from magazines or the Internet avoid celebrities or well-known figures that students can already identify in pop culture or from historic references.

> Facilitator Notes

Modules and activities that addresses an understanding the cultural influences of leadership must attend to the different ways identities and cultures are both visible and invisible. As the above activities address the assumptions students' hold about specific identity and cultural groups, facilitators must also address their own assumptions around identities and cultures. Ideally, the above activities are designed so that no student will feel pressured or forced to reveal any specific social identity or cultural background information that they themselves do not want to share. Facilitators will need to observe and listen for any scenario where other students participating in the activities challenge their fellow students to reveal information that is not willingly shared. There are great benefits from exploring intrapersonal and interpersonal dynamics of cultural influences of leadership, but there is also the possibility of great risk and vulnerability for students and facilitators.

Stephanie H. Chang is a doctoral candidate in the College Student Personnel Program at the University of Maryland, College Park. She is also a graduate coordinator for the minor in leadership studies.

Active Learning Module 5d

Leadership and Communication

Kathryn A. Sturtevant

> Summary of Concepts

This learning module addresses a portion of Chapter 5, Understanding Others. In this section, students learn about leadership and communication concepts. It is essential for students to understand and appreciate difference, as well as develop the skills necessary to lead and communicate with diverse groups. Students should explore how they can increase their multicultural competence to engage others in an inclusive and empowering leadership process. Understanding how to approach the topic of difference in a sensitive and curious way will promote a space for intentional learning and growth.

> Learning Outcomes

Students will

- Understand and articulate awareness of intercultural sensitivity
- Identify and explore various ways to address sensitive multicultural challenges
- Apply inclusive communication techniques

> Module Overview

Students engage in individual reflection in small and large group discussions centered on acknowledging, appreciating, and respecting difference. Students share with a partner and then common themes are addressed in the large group. Students then participate in an activity that challenges them to think critically on how they would respond to sensitive multicultural situations. Students can utilize skills developed throughout their leadership journey.

Estimated Time

Activity 1: Reflection of Intercultural Self-Awareness: Reflect, Pair and Share, 20 minutes

Activity 2: Inclusive Case Study in Small and Large Group Discussion, 40 minutes

Materials/Supplies

Paper and pens/markers for individual reflections

Flip chart

Exploring Leadership (3rd edition) to refer to specific information

Copies of the four scenarios for the Inclusive Case Study activity (provided)

> Module Activities

Activity 1: Reflection of Intercultural Self-Awareness

Time: 20 minutes

Ask students to look up Milton Bennett's Developmental Model of Intercultural Sensitivity depicted in the text (or provide handouts). For the first five minutes, ask students to reflect on where they believe they would fall on the model. Specifically, what comments resonate with them? What experiences have they had or not had that contributed to the stage in which they identify?

Next, ask students to find a partner and share their thoughts from the reflection activity. Encourage students to partner with someone they do not know well. Provide 10 minutes for this section, with each person having five minutes to share. Encourage students to be vulnerable and share specific examples.

Finally, ask partners to come back to large group and seek volunteers to share themes that emerged. On a flip chart, write down key words that summarize the student voice. The purpose of this is to demonstrate common ground among the group when exploring personal stages of understanding about difference. This also acts as a way to affirm where each individual is in their level of understanding, as well as reiterate the need for increased multicultural competence.

Variation   If you have a small, intimate group, you can skip the Pair and Share and jump right into the group discussion. This works well within a cohort of students who have had a history of shared experiences relating to diversity and inclusivity.

Activity 2: Inclusive Case Study

Time: 40 minutes

This activity focuses on information students gained regarding the role of empathy in communication as well as unassertive, assertive and aggressive communication. Direct students to review Exhibit 5.4, Illustrations of Unassertive, Assertive, and Aggressive Communication in their text (or provide handouts). Encourage students to think about these concepts when engaging in this next activity.

Divide students into four groups. Pass out one scenario to each group and ask students to write down their plan of action. While each student may have their own approach, encourage group dialogue and collective responses. Challenge students to also formulate the rationale to back up their plan of action. Allow 10 minutes.

Bring small groups back together and ask one volunteer from each group to read out loud the case study and the group's plan of action. Encourage groups to identify and acknowledge identities that were depicted in each scenario. Dedicate 30 minutes for group discussion and debrief.

Debrief Questions

- What kind of a response did you provide—unassertive, assertive, or aggressive?
- What potential ways can the other person take your response?
- How can the relationships in the case study be used to benefit the outcome?
- What are the assumptions you and your group had about characters in this study? How did those assumptions assist or hinder your conversations?
- How did you employ empathy in your response?
- What are the consequences and/or benefits of your response?
- How did your own identities have a role in shaping your response?

> Facilitator Notes

During small groups for the Inclusive Case Study Activity, it may be beneficial to visit each group to ensure they are thinking critically about the situation—specifically, addressing assumptions, gaining clarification, breaking down stereotypes, acknowledging different perspectives, and so forth.

While groups are sharing their plans of action, encourage other groups to add to the plan. This reinforces the concept that there is not just one way of responding to challenging multicultural situations.

Remind students that curiosity is essential to greater understanding, and by asking appropriate questions to gain new information in an effort to positively influence others they are engaging in an inclusive leadership process.

> Inclusive Case Studies

Scenario 1: You are involved in a student organization that wants to organize a Christmas party before winter break. You notice that not everyone identifies as Christian, and you recommend having a general holiday party instead of focusing specifically on a Christmas-themed party. Another student leader says, "It doesn't really matter too much, because we always have a Christmas party, and if someone doesn't want to attend, they don't have to." The group proceeds to discuss buying a Christmas tree, food options, gift exchange plans, popular Christmas music to play, and so on. How would you handle this situation?

Scenario 2: You are part of a group that plans a large-scale service event in the community. This event typically involves physical labor. You are in charge of recruiting and coordinating all volunteers. One volunteer sends you an email sharing that he is a new student on campus and is really excited to participate in the event this year. He also shares that he is in a wheelchair and will need special accommodations in order to participate. While your email is open, another student reads the email and says, "Oh, don't worry about that. Just tell him that this event involves physical activity, so he won't be able to participate. He should understand." How would you handle this situation?

Scenario 3: You are the treasurer for a student organization. After making an announcement at a meeting about paying dues, $40.00, several students come up to you asking for an extension, or the option of a payment plan. They share that they are not in a financial state to pay up front, but would really like to continue

their involvement with the organization. You decide on a payment plan and all is well. The next day, another student leader informs you that for the committee retreat, everyone needs to pay $100.00 within three days to pay for all up front costs. If students are unable to do so, they will not be allowed to attend. You share with that individual the situation regarding the students who were unable to pay dues, and the student says, "That's not my problem. Ask them just to borrow money from their parents, or they can't go." How would you handle this situation?

Scenario 4: During one of your organization's retreats, you play an icebreaker game that involves female members "quizzing" male members about the things they find attractive about the opposite sex, and vice versa. For example, a male will get in the middle of the circle and the female members will shout questions about dating, relationships, and so forth regarding the opposite sex.

This game is somewhat of a tradition for this organization and every year the questions get more and more personal. You know a few of the new members identify as gay and lesbian. When you approach another student leader about your discomfort putting students who identify as gay and lesbian in a potentially oppressive environment, their response is, "It's just a game. It really isn't that big of a deal and this one game shouldn't really matter." How would you handle this situation?

Kathryn A. Sturtevant is a student development specialist and advisor for the Leadership & Service Center within the Department of Student Activities at Texas A&M University. Kathryn received her MA in higher education administration from the University of Denver and specializes in helping students understand and appreciate the connections between diversity, social justice, and leadership development.

Active Learning Module 6a

Creating and Sustaining an Ethical Organizational Environment

Wendy Wagner

> ## Summary of Concepts

This learning module addresses a portion of Chapter 6. This section delves deeper into the discussion of the importance of ethics in the practice of leadership. Topics include the process of creating and sustaining ethical organizational environments, an analysis of the moral dimensions of transforming leadership theory, and an examination of the ethical influences that participants have on their organizations through behavior modeling. Readers are exposed to aspects of bad leadership, the perils of having ethical lapses, and the importance of moral courage in practicing ethical leadership.

> ## Learning Outcomes

Students will

- Learn to identify ethical issues in organizational settings in order to frame them for group members
- Be able to analyze how an organization's processes can influence ethical or unethical behavior from members

- Consider the roles of leaders and followers with respect to ethical lapses and acts of courage
- Learn to be mindful of how an organization's values and ethical standards are communicated to members and how new members are socialized into the group from an ethical vantage point

> Module Overview

In this module, students in small groups are given a pair of organization values and asked to create a scenario in which those two values clash, creating an ethical dilemma for group leaders and members to navigate. As these scenarios are discussed in the large group, students are encouraged to make connections to issues brought up in the chapter, including the way organizational culture fosters ethical or unethical behavior and the role of leaders and group members in creating ethical group environments. Finally, students consider how organizational values are communicated in their own groups.

Estimated Time
Activity 1: The Clash of the Values, 15-minute activity in small groups

Activity 2: Leaders Create Environments, 30-minute large group sharing and discussion

Activity 3: Communicating Group Values, 15-minute discussion

Materials/Supplies
Value pairs (suggestions below) printed on cards to share with groups

> Module Activities

Activity 1: The Clash of the Values

Time: 15 minutes

Begin by framing ethical issues as a clash of two or more equally held values, as opposed to moral issues, which are issues of right versus wrong. Explain that individuals often wrestle with ethical issues (provide some examples, such as loyalty and kindness to a friend versus being honest with them about a fair critique). In today's activity they will explore ethical issues from a whole-group perspective—when an organization's shared values clash.

Divide into three to four small groups (adjust number of groups to the number of participants, but keep in mind the time you will have for each group to report out). Provide each small group a different set of conflicting organizational values. Adjust these values to those the group will find relevant given their campus roles and recent issues on campus and in the news. Some examples include

- Address local community needs through community service *and* be inclusive of ideas and input from all members
- Uphold stated standards of responsible behavior *and* serve as the primary social outlet for group members
- Maintain a high standard for good grades among group members *and* adhere to the campus honor code
- Meet the group mission to provide a campus programming tradition *and* follow all university policies
- Create a welcoming safe space for students from marginalized groups *and* advocate for better campus representation of people from those marginalized groups
- Be the "best" campus organization (self-defined: most popular, win most awards, win most sporting events, etc.) *and* demonstrate respect for students in other organizations

Instruct the groups to create a fictional scenario, in the context of a campus or community organization they find relevant, in which these values clash with each other. They should try to include as many details as possible and consider the roles of multiple people in and outside of the organization. Groups may struggle at first, as there are many scenarios in which both values can be attended to. Suggest that sometimes the seeming inability to attend to both values arises from unexpected limitations, like being short on time or resources or having an unexpected challenge arise, that make it seem difficult to accommodate both values so groups choose one or the other—usually the path of least resistance. Sometimes situations present an imbalance such that a seemingly small violation of one value would result in a huge gain in the other value.

Students should prepare to present this scenario to the large group in a creative way. For example, they could have a talk show host describe the situation and then interview each person involved for his or her perspective. Or they could present the scene as a reality TV show episode, with interactive scenes and individual "confessional" scenes from each person involved in the situation.

Activity 2: Leaders Create Environments

Time: 30 minutes

After each small group presents their case, discuss the following issues as they are relevant to the case:

1. What were the clashing values in this scenario?
2. What aspects of the scenario created a situation that tempted members to be unethical?

    Several factors can create a press on members to make unethical choices. Any number of these might come up as you discuss the scenarios.

    • Incredibly competitive environments. When people will do anything to win, or feel like the rewards for winning vastly outweigh the risk of being unethical, the organization may actually press typically ethical people to do unethical acts.

- Incredibly achievement focused organizations. The rewards for achievement convince people that small "cheats" along the way are worth it (we *must* have good grades or the perfect campus event at all costs).
- Short time frames to achieve goals. When people have a big task and not enough time to do it, shortcuts often involve sacrificing one value for another.
- Focus on policies and laws over values and principles. People can easily come up with ways to stay within the letter of the law even if they aren't abiding by the spirit of the law.
- Evaluation based purely on results. "Success" needs to also factor in having had a good process, such that members and stakeholders felt included and valued. Avoid a bottom-line mentality.

3. How can organization leaders influence an ethical organization environment in this case?

4. What is the role of the organization member in supporting ethical organization environments? What should be the expectation of members to hold leaders accountable?

5. What connections can be made between this scenario and Nash's (1990) four qualities for participants to advance ethical standards in groups:

- Critical thinking skills to analyze and convey the ethical components of a problem or dilemma
- Possessing a high degree of integrity to stand up for your personal and professional ethics
- The ability to see situations from others' perspectives (showing concern for others)
- Being personally motivated to do the right thing (pp. 43–47)

Activity 3: Communicating Group Values

Time: 15 minutes

Ask students how these clashing values play out in the groups they are a part of. What other values are often at odds in their groups? What is the organizational climate in relation to group members holding leaders accountable to ethical standards in behavior and decision-making?

Ask students how their group's values are communicated. How are new members socialized to "the way things are done here?" Challenge them to go beyond the "official" statements of standards to examining how leaders and older members model acceptable behavior and how the rewards structures communicate what is most important. Have them consider how these rewards can be both formal, such as "member of the year," and informal, such as the most popular group member.

Have students consider the role of storytelling. Almost all groups have celebrated stories that get passed on from older members to newer ones. The story of how the group got started is one example, as are stories about "legendary" members. For example, are stories told about the group members who achieved at all costs? Are stories shared about the time the group did the right thing even though they didn't "win the day?" Do a group's stories demonstrate pride in an ongoing sense of honor over one-time achievements? Have students share some of the stories from their groups and consider them in light of the group values they convey.

❯ References

Nash, L. L. (1990). *Good intentions aside*. Boston, MA: Harvard Business School Press.

Wendy Wagner is an assistant professor of leadership and community engagement at George Mason University. She is also the director of Mason's Center for Leadership and Community Engagement.

Active Learning Module 6b

Assumptions About Ethical Leadership

Daniel Ostick

> Summary of Concepts

This learning module addresses a portion of Chapter 6, Leading with Integrity. In this section, students consider eight assumptions about leadership:

- Ethics is the heart of leadership
- All leadership is values-driven
- Personal values intersect with organizational values
- Ethical leadership can be learned
- Ethical leadership involves a connection between ethical thought and action
- Character development is an essential ingredient of ethical leadership
- Ethical leadership is a shared process
- Everything we do teaches

Ethics exist in a cultural and temporal context. What is considered ethical in one culture or period may be different for another culture or at a different time. Some authors have asserted that there are common ethical values across cultures, such as love, truthfulness, fairness, freedom, unity, tolerance, responsibility, and respect for life. Others have suggested that there are common virtues, such as wisdom and knowledge, courage, love, and humanity, justice, temperance, and spirituality and transcendence. While definitions may vary, the basic ideals are similar.

> Learning Outcomes

Students will

- Identify their own assumptions about leadership and compare these to the text and other students
- Consider cultural dimensions of leadership in relationship to personal culture

> Overview of the Module

Small groups of students are each assigned to discuss one of eight statements about ethical leadership. As they report out to the larger group, the way each statement corresponds to one of the eight "assumptions about leadership" from the chapter emerges. Students will explore common beliefs and contrasting beliefs between each other and the authors.

Finally, students reflect upon and share some of the way their cultural background has shaped their assumptions about leadership. Culture here is considered broadly in terms of many aspects of social identity.

Estimated time

Activity 1: Assumptions About Leadership, 10-minute small group exploration, 20 minute large group discussion

Activity 2: Cultural Assumptions, 5-minute individual reflection, 25-minute discussion

Materials/Supplies

Board or flip charts with markers to write down major points emerging from the discussion

> Module Activities

Activity 1: Assumptions About Leadership

Time: 25–30 minutes

Divide students into eight groups (if a smaller set of students, you can divide them into four groups and have each group explore two assumptions). Give each group one statement that corresponds to an assumption listed in the text. Use the following statements, but do not initially share which assumption to which they correspond:

- Leadership can be "good" even if it isn't ethical. (for assumption 1)
- Leadership can be value-neutral. (for assumption 2)
- It's OK if your personal values don't align with your organization. (for assumption 3)
- People cannot learn to be more ethical. (for assumption 4)
- You can be ethical and sometimes do unethical things. (for assumption 5)
- You must walk the talk. (for assumption 6)
- Ethics are most powerful when given to an organization by its positional leader. (for assumption 7)
- People will understand if I do something unethical if it's for good reasons. (for assumption 8)

Ask each group to discuss their statement and then share with the larger group. Facilitation points for each statement to explore include

- Leadership can be "good" even if it isn't ethical. (for assumption 1)

- Do we usually think of ethics when we discuss leadership, or do we focus more on results, outcomes, and effectiveness?
- Is leadership better when it's ethical? Are ethics *more* important than outcomes?
- Leadership can be value-neutral. (for assumption 2)
  - What kinds of leadership might be value-neutral?
  - Do we use ethics at all times? Can we be ethics-neutral or do we always carry a point of view?
- It's OK if your personal values don't align with your organization. (for assumption 3)
  - What impact does nonalignment have on you? On your organization?
  - How can you find out if an organization has values that match yours?
  - Does everyone in an organization need to agree on what is ethical?
- People cannot learn to be more ethical. (for assumption 4)
  - Do you have an example of a time when you learned from doing something unethical?
  - When is the last time you discussed ethics with friends? Family? Anyone?
  - Can you learn ethics on your own?
- You can be ethical and do unethical things. (for assumption 5)
  - "But I am a good person" and "My actions don't define me" are sometimes said to show this contrast. How tied are ethics to actions?
  - When have you been faced with an ethical choice?
- You must walk the talk. (for assumption 6)
  - Do you know anyone you don't think is ethical? What impact does that have on your relationship? If in an organization, what impact does it have on the organization?
- Ethics are most powerful when given to an organization by its positional leader. (for assumption 7)

- In your groups, do you ever talk about the groups' ethical values or statements?
- Who is responsible for making sure members of a group are ethical? How do they do this?
- People will understand if I do something unethical if it's for good reasons (for assumption 8).
  - Some espouse the "newspaper rule" to determine ethical behavior. How would you feel if your actions were printed in your hometown newspaper? Do you think this is a fair measure?
  - "Everyone else does it" is sometimes said to justify behaviors. Have you been a part of an organization where unethical behavior has seeped into the organization?

Variations on Activity   You can also treat this activity as a continuum exercise. Read a statement from the list and have students line up in the room according to whether they agree with the statement (at one end) or disagree (at the other) or fall somewhere along the continuum. Use the facilitation questions to explore in more depth.

Activity 2: Cultural Assumptions

Time: 30 minutes

Lead the group in a quick "popcorn" activity. Ask the group as a whole to shout out (like popping popcorns) their cultures. There is no need to define "cultures" at this point. Anything they shout out is fine. As they share, you may want to write the items down as a visual reminder. Items might include different nationalities, races, genders, sexual orientations, religions, and so forth. Ask the group if they think all these cultures would agree about what is or is not "ethical."

Ask each student to get out a piece of paper and write down one aspect of his or her culture, background, or identity that has influenced his or her beliefs about leadership, and to write down how. After a few minutes, have students pair up with someone they do not know and share this item.

Engage the group in a discussion about the issues raised. Keep in mind that students may not feel comfortable sharing personal items with the larger group, so do not ask everyone to share and do not call on individual students. Ask for volunteers. As students share, the facilitation should tie the pieces together:

- Did anyone else have a similar item? (or an item related to a similar cultural identity?)
- Do you think other cultures or identities received a contrasting message? Do you know anyone from those other identities?

Remind the group that a future module (see module on Ethical Decision Making) will help them think more about how culture and identity influence the decisions they make or dilemmas they face.

> Facilitator Notes

This module will be most useful when paired with the module on Ethical Decision Making to tie together students' beliefs about ethics with practical applications.

Be prepared for students to share ideas like "all ethics are subjective, so how can we really say something is or is not ethical?" With a conversation about cultural dimensions of leadership, the goal is not to decide what is good and bad, but to explore how ethics and culture intersect and to understand and contrast.

You should also be prepared for students to have very different assumptions about leadership. While trying to come to a group consensus about why ethics is important to leadership may be a powerful exercise, this module is to help students see their personal beliefs about ethics in comparison to others.

Daniel Ostick is the coordinator for leadership curriculum development and academic partnerships in the Adele H. Stamp Student Union–Center for Campus Life at the University of Maryland. Daniel received his PhD in college student personnel at the University of Maryland with a research focus on leadership development and LGBT identity and his master's degree in college student personnel administration from Indiana University.

Active Learning Module 6c

Ethical Decision Making

Nick Lennon

> Summary of Concepts

This learning module addresses aspects of Chapter 6, Leading with Integrity, that are related to ethical decision making. We all make decisions about what is right or wrong, good or bad, every day. Ethical leaders should stop to reflect on how ethical decisions are made. They need to understand diverse viewpoints and empower other individuals and groups to behave ethically. This module discusses ethical decision-making models that can help leaders to move beyond self-interest to consider other individuals, groups, and the world as a whole.

> Learning Outcomes

Students will

- Be able to articulate how they currently make decisions about what is ethical or unethical
- Consider alternative ways of making ethical decisions through reflection, listening, and discussion
- Apply ethical theories to various ethical scenarios

> Module Overview

Students reflect on what ethics means to them and then participate in a four-corners activity designed to uncover how they currently make decisions about a series of statements, particularly ones that address "right versus right" decisions (as mentioned in Chapter 6 of *Exploring Leadership*, 3rd edition). Students hear diverse viewpoints from their peers about how they each decide what is ethical or unethical. Students then learn about alternative ways to make ethical decisions and consider how their current decision-making processes match up or do not match up with ethical decision-making models and theories discussed in Chapter 6.

Estimated Time
- Activity 1: What is Ethics? 10-minute discussion and video clip
- Activity 2: Ethical Decision Making Four Corners, 35-minute activity
- Activity 3: Connection to Theory, 15-minute large group discussion

Materials/Supplies
Technology to project online video clip

Board or flip charts with markers to write down major points emerging from the discussion

A video clip of the TV show *The Office* (Season 5, Episode 2: "Business Ethics")

Signs for the four corners of the room: strongly agree, agree, disagree, strongly disagree

List of ethical decision statements

> Module Activities

Activity 1: What Is Ethics?

Time: 10 minutes

Ask students what ideas pop into their minds when they hear the word "ethics?" Give students time to write on a sheet of paper ("What is ethics?").

Show a video clip of the TV show *The Office* (Season 5, Episode 2: "Business Ethics"). Show the clip from when Holly says, "Pencils down!" until Oscar says: "That isn't ethics. Ethics is a real discussion of the competing conceptions of the good. This is just the corporate anti-shoplifting rules." It is possible to substitute this clip with any clip where the characters exhibit a common misconception about ethics.

Ask students how the word *ethics* is perceived by the characters in the clip and how that is similar or different to what the students wrote or said earlier. Explain that this discussion was designed to get a sense of what images/ideas they associate with the word *ethics*, since there are different ideas about ethics, and that it is not just a series of rules telling them what not to do.

Discuss the definition of ethics from Chapter 6. Emphasize ethical decision making as discerning one's options between two conflicting values, or "right" versus "right."

Activity 2: Ethical Decision Making Four Corners

Time: 35 minutes

Open this activity by describing decision-making as something that people do not always engage in with conscious thought. This activity is designed to uncover our often subconscious rational for ethical decisions.

Following a statement, students will move to one corner of the room to indicate whether they strongly agree, agree, disagree, or strongly disagree. They must move to one area, not in between two areas. Ask students to try their best to move based on what *they* honestly feel they would most likely *do* in the situations and to try not to move based solely on social pressures to portray themselves in a certain way in front of the rest of the group. Finally, ask students to be pay attention to what emotions they feel during this activity (e.g., which questions/comments "push their buttons") and to be respectful, since the statements can be emotional for some people.

Read a statement. Once students have moved to the various corners of the room, ask students in each area to

1. Identify what the competing values in this decision are for them
2. Articulate what reasoning they used to choose between the competing values

If students have previously identified their values in an earlier activity, ask if their choice matches with their values. Ask the students to stick to "I" statements and to respond to you, the facilitator. Keep in mind that each one of the statements could lead to an in-depth discussion, so you may need to intervene to move the discussion along.

Suggested Statements

- I just signed an honor code pledge agreeing to abide by academic honesty policies, including any witnessing of cheating incidents. My best friend is in my accounting course and I observe that friend cheating during an in-class exam. I would report my friend. (*Note:* This statement is from the first page of Chapter 6.)

- Variations for follow-up discussion: What if the person you observed cheating was a stranger? What if it was someone you really did not like? Is there a difference in how you would respond? Why or why not?

  Note: This question gets at Kidder's (2005) "Truth versus Loyalty" dilemma paradigm, mentioned in Chapter 6.

- I am taking care of my friend's cat while my friend is on vacation. One day, about halfway into my friend's vacation, I walk into my friend's place to discover that his pet cat has died. I would wait until my friend got back from the trip to tell him.

- If my friend is joining a student organization and I know she is being hazed (it may be necessary to define hazing for some students), but the friend asks me not to tell. I would still tell someone who could have an impact on stopping the hazing.

- If I saw a homeless person begging on the street, I would give him money.

- If a good friend just bought an expensive outfit and asks me if I like it (and I think it's awful) I would share my true feelings with that friend.

- I would purchase tickets to a concert that I had no interest in so that I can sell them online for a profit.

- I would continue to eat chicken if I knew that the chicken I was eating came from a farm that had horrible, but sanitary, conditions for the animals.

  - Variations for follow-up discussion: What about pork? Beef? Fish? What is the difference, if any?

- I would speak up if I heard someone that I do not know make an offensive ethnic slur at a party.

- If I discover that a good friend is cheating on his or her partner and I am also very close to that partner, I would tell that partner about my discovery of the affair.

- I have been waiting for about eight minutes in a long line of traffic during rush hour, waiting to merge onto another street. A car pulls up next to me and the driver has their blinker on, trying to get over into my lane. I would allow the driver to pull in front of me.

- Variation for follow-up discussion: What if you were late to work? What if the day before, you tried to do the same thing because you got caught in the wrong lane and did not realize the line of cars started so far back?

You can find many more statements from the game *Scruples* (Scruples by Milton Bradley: http://www.scruplesgame .com/main.html) or through an online search. Make sure to select questions that get at right versus right decisions as mentioned in the chapter, not just right versus wrong decisions.

Debrief Discussion   People often make decisions without much conscious thought. Can practice help a person learn to more automatically consider ethics in their decision-making?

Ask students about how culture and identity influence the decisions they make. What is one aspect of your culture, background, or identity that has influenced your beliefs about what is ethical? Do you feel that there are universal values that apply across cultures? Why or why not?

Additional discussion questions:

- What stood out to you about this activity?
- What statements/situations were more emotional for you? Why?
- What surprised you about this activity?
- Were there any patterns to where people were standing at different times?
- For those of you who stood relatively alone at some point, what did it feel like to be standing apart from others?
- What explanation (reasoning) did you hear that you really liked?

- Did this exercise force you to think about anything? What?
- How does this exercise relate to being a student?
- How does this exercise relate to being a person in the world in general?
- How does this exercise relate to leadership?
- What did you learn from this activity?

Activity 3: Connection to Theory

Time: 15 minutes

Reiterate that the four-corners activity was meant to help students uncover the reasons that they may currently use to make ethical decisions and to expose them to other reasons. Explain that we all are already using certain reasons (including our "gut reaction" or "intuition") for different actions and we may or may not be conscious of them. Continual reflection can help us learn to be consciously aware of our *reasons* when we make decisions, so we can be more intentional about them.

At this point, without calling out individual students, you can share some statements that you heard during the four corners activity (e.g., "it just feels right," "it wouldn't be fair," "it would be best for greatest number of people") to highlight different ideas that the students consider when of making decisions. Have students share the thoughts that occur to them as they are trying to make decisions, for example, "How would I want to be treated in that situation?" or "Would I be comfortable with this decision being on the front-page news?" If they are unable to remember what they ask themselves when trying to make decisions, ask them to think back to the four-corners activity and a reason they used for why they were standing where they were standing for one of the statements.

Review Kidder's Nine Checkpoints for dealing with ethical issues (cited in Chapter 6). Ask the students which of Kidder's

Resolution Principles (from Chapter 6) they find themselves using most often (e.g., ends-based, rules-based, care-based) and what might be some pros and cons of their personal approach. For example, a potential con of the ends-based approach is that if they only focus on the consequence of their actions they may not focus as much on the process it took to get there. You can also discuss concepts such as the Golden Rule, which is listed under "care-based thinking."

Encourage students to continue to reflect on how they can use all three of Kidder's Resolution Principles: ends-based, rules-based, and care-based.

Variation　　If there is time or if the group needs to warm up to the discussion, you can divide the group into pairs and ask them to discuss what reasons they find themselves using in daily life and/or in the four-corners activity.

> Facilitator Notes

If you have already conducted a "values clarification" activity with this group of students, it is helpful to encourage students to consider this discussion to be an extension of that one as it considers decision-making when two values conflict (right versus right).

During the four-corners activity students may ask for more details about each statement, but it is important to tell them that they should use their own interpretation of each statement.

The four-corners activity may bring up strong emotions for some students because it can tap into deep beliefs and create cognitive dissonance (e.g., a student enjoys eating chicken but is not sure of the conditions of the farm where those chickens are raised and they feel guilty, defensive). It is very important to create a safe environment where students have a sense of trust so that they can be honest, really examine what they believe, and be open to hearing diverse viewpoints.

❯ Reference

Kidder, R. M. (2005). *Moral courage: Taking action when your values are put to the test*. New York, NY: William Morrow.

Nick Lennon is the director of the Leadership Education and Development (LEAD) Office at George Mason University. He received his PhD in educational psychology from the University of Texas at Austin and focuses on infusing ethical development into leadership initiatives.

What Is Community and Why Is It Important?

Kathleen Callahan

> Summary of Concepts

This learning module addresses the first portion of Chapter 7, Being in Communities. In this section, students explore the importance of community and the elements of community. In college and university life, we are involved in many different communities, from our business fraternity to our living learning community to our intramural team. Why are these communities important and what makes them effective? Gardner (1990) outlines eight elements that define effective communities:

1. Wholeness incorporating diversity
2. A shared culture
3. Good internal communication
4. Caring, trust, and teamwork
5. Group maintenance and governance
6. Participation and shared leadership tasks
7. Development of young people (or new members)
8. Links with the outside world

> Learning Outcomes

Students will

- Consider how privilege influences their lives and the communities they belong to
- Relate theory to practice through personal experiences and film
- Be able to articulate the differences between communities they belong to that are effective and those that are not, according to Gardner's eight elements of effective communities

> Module Overview

Students participate in a privilege walk activity and engage in open dialogue about privilege and diversity and how they impact community. Students then relate Gardner's eight elements to film clips and identify effective community within the film. Students reflect on communities in which they belong and identify what makes them effective or not effective, based on Gardner's eight elements, and share those experiences in small groups.

Estimated Time

Activity 1: Privilege Walk, 10-minute activity, 30-minute discussion

Activity 2: Film Connection to Theory, 10-minute viewing, 10-minute discussion

Materials/Supplies

Technology to project video clips

Board or flip charts with markers to write down points emerging from discussion

List of Privilege statements

> Module Activities

Activity 1: Privilege Walk and Debrief Discussion

Time: 40 minutes

(Modified from multiple diversity and privilege resources from *Winthrop University Diversity Manual* and Colorado State Human Issues Programming)

Diversity is a major component of community, and it is important for students to be able to openly discuss the topic in a safe environment. Privilege and diversity impacts community and how we form our worldview and experiences. This activity will help students understand that privilege plays an important role in community.

This topic can be sensitive and challenging for students. Set ground rules:

1. Students are to be silent throughout the activity.
2. This activity is voluntary and students can choose not to move if they are uncomfortable.
3. Any other established rules that you feel necessary or pertinent.

This activity should be done outside or in a classroom large enough for students to stand side by side in a single line. Start with the class in a single line (shoulder to shoulder or holding hands, whatever is most comfortable for your students). Read the following statements slowly and leave a moment of silence after each statement for students to reflect. This activity can be modified with other statements appropriate to the topic of privilege and diversity.

- If your parents are or were professionals: doctors, lawyers, take one step forward
- If you attended private school or summer camp, take one step forward

- If you were ever called names because of your race, class, ethnicity, gender, or sexual orientation, take one step back
- If your hometown had opportunities to engage in cultural experiences such as concerts, live theater or art galleries, take one step forward
- If your place of work or school is closed on your major religious holidays, take one step forward
- If you had to rely primarily on public transportation, take one step back
- If you can openly show affection for your partner without fear of harassment or assault, take one step forward
- If you saw members of your race, ethnic group, gender, or sexual orientation portrayed on television in degrading roles, take one step back
- If you can go to a clothing store and find clothes in your size easily, take one step forward
- If your first language is spoken in most places you go, take one step forward
- If your dietary needs are met at most public locations, take one step forward
- If you were ever afraid of violence because of your race, ethnicity, gender, or sexual orientation, take one step back
- If you ever inherited money or property, take one step forward
- If your parents did not grow up in the United States, take one step back
- If your parents told you could be anything you wanted to be, take one step forward
- If you ever had to skip a meal or were hungry because there was not enough money to buy food when you were growing up, take one step back
- If you do not have to worry where curb cuts are located because you are able-bodied, take one step forward
- If your ancestors were forced to come to the United States, not by choice, take one step back

- If growing up you had more than 100 books at home, take one step forward
- If you were ever ashamed or embarrassed of your clothes, house, car, take one step back
- If your elementary school included the study of the culture of your ancestors, take one step forward
- If you ever tried to change your appearance, mannerisms, or behavior to avoid being judged or ridiculed, take one step back
- If you were told that you were smart and capable by your parents, take one step forward
- If your gender is often used as a sex object in the media, take a step forward

Have students look around and reflect on where they are standing in relation to others or those with stretched arms (if still holding hands) before sitting back down.

Debrief Discussion Questions
- What are your thoughts on this activity?
- Reflect on the questions. Did any statements surprise you or make you uncomfortable?
- What types of privilege and diversity were parts of this activity (race, gender, sexual orientation, ability, socioeconomic status, weight, upbringing)? Was anything missing?
- Did some of the statements feel unfair? How did you feel about where you stood in relation to others?
- How does this relate to privilege and diversity in our communities (college, city/town, state, nation, and world communities)?
- What privilege do we have as a whole group that others may not? (Living in the United States, being in college, and so forth.)
- How can we use these differences and privileges to benefit others in our community?

Discussion: Connections to Chapter 7 Students can discuss the connections between the Privilege Walk activity and Chapter 7 either in small groups or as a whole.

- To what extent do you consider any of the social identity groups connected to this activity (gender, ethnicity, social class, sexual orientation, among others) to be a community that you belong to?
  - How is this definition of community similar to and different from other perspectives on "community," such as community that involves people who are geographically connected?
  - Do any of these groups represent a "community of practice" for you?
- What are your other communities of practice?
- In what ways are these social identities represented in the communities that are most central to you?
- In what ways do you benefit from community?
- In what ways to you contribute to community?
- How would you respond to some of these assertions from Chapter Seven in light of the Privilege Walk activity?
  - "A true community cannot exist without diversity" (Gudykunst, 1991, p. 146).
  - To value community is to value our interdependence.
  - In Chapter 7, Martin Buber's description of communities is of a group of people who have made a choice around a common center, "A true community is not a collection of people who all think alike but people with differing minds and complementary natures."

Variation You may consider contacting campus diversity educators to facilitate this or a similar activity.

Activity 2: Film Connection to Theory

Time: 20 minutes

View these video clips from *Remember the Titans* (Bruckheimer, Oman, Howard, & Yakin, 2000):

- Chapter 5 and 6 (14:21 to 20:00)—first clip
- Chapter 9 and 10 (29:09 to 36:56)—second clip

Discuss the following questions (either in small groups or as a whole):

- What does the first clip show? What kind of community is represented? Which of Gardner's eight elements are present/missing?
- What does the second clip show? Which of Gardner's eight elements are present/missing?
- What took place from clip one to clip two?
- How can Gudykunst's (1991) seven community building principles be applied?

› Facilitator Notes

Be prepared for a wide range of leadership issues to surface here. This can be a great day to refer back to in subsequent workshops or courses as it provides common language for a host of complex ideas that emerge as students gain a deeper understanding of leadership issues. The topic of privilege can be sensitive. If you feel your class is not well connected or mature enough to handle it, make adjustments to statements with other appropriate material.

> References

Bruckheimer, J. (Producer) Oman, C. (Producer) Howard, G. A. (Writer) & Yakin, B. (Director). (2000). *Remember the titans* [DVD]. Walt Disney Pictures and Jerry Bruckheimer Films.

Buber, M. (1958). *I and thou.* New York, NY: Scribner.

Gudykunst, W. B. (1991). *Bridging differences: Effective intergroup communication.* Thousand Oaks, CA: Sage.

Kathleen Callahan is a PhD student in higher education administration at Florida State University. She serves a dual role as the Certificate in Undergraduate Leadership Studies advisor and the Higher Education Program graduate assistant.

Active Learning Module 7b

Community Building

Laura McMaster

> Summary of Concepts

This learning module addresses the first portion of Chapter 7, Being in Communities. In this section, students learn about the four stages of developing authentic community. All organizations, indeterminate of their goals, engage in a similar developmental process. As is the case with stage theories, it is important to make clear that it is not the end that is most important, but instead the process of achieving those ends. Most groups will start out as a pseudocommunity and although some might progress to the other stages, potentially landing within authenticity, it is also just as likely that some groups may remain in the initial stage, unable or unwilling to continue.

Furthermore, there are seven principles of community building that individuals can engage in to become more effective members of their community. These principles assert that members who are dedicated and practice community-building skills will enrich the organization.

> Learning Outcomes

Students will

- Be able to identify their own communities and how they contribute to them
- Understand the challenges and opportunities created within community building

> Module Overview

The first activity is a simulation exercise in which two groups with different assigned "cultural norms" interact in order to meet a goal. The second activity engages students in collaboration across assigned groups to construct a Lego® airplane.

Estimated Time
Activity 1: Saving Civilization, 30 minutes
Activity 2: Lego My Airplane, 15-minute activity, 15-minute reflective discussion

Materials/Supplies
Stack of paper
A bundle of pens
Tape (multiple rolls)
Printed out civilization guides
Legos

> Module Activities

Activity 1: Saving Civilization

Time: 30 minutes
For groups of 30 or less, divide into two groups. Ask for two to four volunteers to serve as observers. For larger groups,

you may choose to divide into four groups. Separate the groups, preferably sending one group into a hallway or another room.

Group A is given the following instructions: Please note that you can change these instructions to fit the needs of the group. Assign one to two observers to this group and have them take notes on what they see happen.

You are all members of the planet Collegies. As members of this civilization, you have learned to act and communicate in specific ways, including

- When you walk up to someone and wish to start a conversation you must do a very bold and obvious wave gesture accompanied by a loud greeting of some sort.
- During conversation you will continuously try to tango with your conversational partner, as your civilization feels more comfortable in the tango position.
- Conversation topics that you feel comfortable with are paper, pens, and tape, especially since these are the items that sustain your civilization's way of life.
- Conversation topics that make you feel uncomfortable include plates, forks, and cups. When you hear these words you immediately yodel for three seconds before reemerging in the conversation.
- The word *like* is considered culturally offensive to you. When you hear the word *like* you lightly slap the hand of the person who said the word and inform them in a loud manner not to use that word.
- When you are finished with the conversation, slowly back away from your conversational partner, clapping quickly and loudly.

After group A is given their instruction, they must practice communicating as true members of their civilization. It is of critical importance that they stay in character.

After three to five minutes practicing, you stop the group and tell them the following. The ruler of the planet of Collegies has just called and the future of the entire planet rests on you. Failure to complete this mission will result in total destruction of your home planet. You must travel to the far off planet of Universitus and get their help to obtain the materials your planet needs to survive. The items needed per person are three pieces of paper, two pens, and one inch of tape. Work fast, Collegies is counting on you. You have 1 minute to discuss and strategize a plan.

While Group A is meeting, Group B is given the following instructions:

- When you walk up to someone and you wish to start a conversation you must "oink" like a pig first.
- Once the conversation has begun, you must stay at least two feet away from the person you are talking to at all times.
- Conversation topics that you feel comfortable with include the plates, forks, and spoons.
- Conservation topics that make you feel uncomfortable include paper, pens, and tape. When you hear these words you immediately put your head down, shake it fast, saying "no, no, no, no, no."
- If you really like the person that you are talking to, you will wink excessively at them.
- When talking, you use the word *like* several times.
- When you are finished with the conversation, turn your back to the person you are talking to and "oink" like a pig twice.

After group B is given their instruction, they must practice communicating as true members of their civilization. It is of critical importance that they stay in character. After three to five minutes of practicing, they are told that there is a new civilization that will be joining them. The new group's motives are unknown. They must work together to figure out how to handle the new group coming to join them. They will have one minute to strategize.

After practicing commences, have the two groups meet each other. Allow them to attempt to communicate. Have the observers take notes on what they are seeing.

After three to five minutes give the groups a two-minute warning. At the end of time, ask the students to retake their seats.

Debriefing Questions

- Have each group read out their rules of civilization to the rest of the students.
- What was difficult about this exercise?
- Were you successful in your mission? Why? Why not?
- What did you learn about yourself during this experience?
- How does this apply to the groups that you are a part of throughout campus?
- What are strategies that you could use to further community building?

Activity 2: Lego My Airplane

Time: 30 minutes

Divide students into groups of three or more. Groups can have up to 10 students. After placing students into groups, provide them with a bag of random Legos. Instruct them that they will be given five minutes to create the best airplane that they can.

After five minutes, yell "stop, hands up." Have each group move to the airplane to their right. Give them another five minutes to create the best airplane that they can.

After five minutes, yell "stop, hands up." Have each group move back to their original airplane. Give them three minutes to make any final changes to their airplane. After three minutes, stop them.

Have each group show their creation.

Debriefing Questions
- How well did your group work together to build your airplane?
- What was your reaction when you had to leave your original airplane?
- How did you feel when you came back to your original airplane?
- Did you use effective community building skills to achieve your goal? Explain.
- How could you have been more effective?
- How does this exercise relate to your organizations throughout campus?

Concluding Discussion Review Peck's (1987) four stages of community development and Gudykunst's seven community building principles from Chapter 7 (Gudykunst, 1991). How might you consider your experience in these two simulations through the lenses of these theories? Could these principles have helped you be more effective during the simulations? How does this relate to your experience working in groups within other communities?

> Facilitator Notes

For the airplane activity, the purpose of these questions is to help students realize that they weren't limited to working in their specific groups, they could have built their community in any way that they thought would be most effective.

Also, feel free to elaborate based on the reactions of the groups, that is, if one of the groups completely destroys the work done by another team either when they switch or when they switch back to their original work, talk to them about how that relates to how we work within our own organizations.

> References

Bennis, W. G. (1989). *On becoming a leader*. Reading, MA: Addison-Wesley.

Gudykunst, W. B. (1991). *Bridging differences: Effective intergroup communication*. Thousand Oaks, CA: Sage.

Peck, M. S. (1987). *The different drum: Community-making and peace*. New York, NY: Simon & Schuster.

Laura McMaster is the director of student leadership and engagement at East Carolina University. She has her master of education from the University of Georgia in college student affairs administration.

Active Learning Module 8a

Understanding Groups and Group Development

Melissa Shehane

> Summary of Concepts

This module will address concepts related to Chapter 8, Interacting in Teams and Groups. Many of us have been a part of or interacted in some sort of group. Reflecting upon how groups form and develop over time will help aspiring leaders navigate their roles within group settings. The chapter explores Tuckman's stages of group development: forming, storming, norming, and performing. The chapter also addresses an often missed critical stage in the development process, the adjourning stage.

> Learning Outcomes

Students will

- Be able to identify Tuckman's stages of group development
- Explore strategies that support the adjourning stage of group development

› Module Overview

Students will identify the current stage of development of an actual group they belong to. In small groups, students will discuss the lived reality of that stage and prepare a creative presentation about the stage to share with the large group. To address the important adjourning stage, students will reflect on ways to bring meaningful closure to an organization experience.

Estimated Time
Activity 1: Tuckman's Touch Points, 35 minutes
Activity 2: Adjourning, 10-minute small group discussion,
    15-minute large group sharing

Materials/Supplies
Paper and pens/markers for individual reflections
Flip chart
Exploring Leadership (3rd edition) text to refer students to for
    specific information
Optional: an assortment of items students might use for costumes
    and props to encourage creativity

› Module Activities

Activity 1: Tuckman's Touch Points

Time: 35 minutes
    Ask students to reflect individually about groups in which they have been a member. To help them articulate their learning, prompt the students with the following questions:

* Identify an organization that you have been or are currently a member of.
* Address the three key dimensions of groups from Chapter 8: Interacting in Teams and Groups.

- What are the group's purposes?
- How would you describe its structure?
- What is the length of time the group is intended to exist?
- What stage of development of Tuckman's model do you believe this group is in?
- How do you know that the group is in this stage?
  Allow 5–10 minutes.

Ask students to divide into groups by the stage of Tuckman's model they identified. You may need to adjust groups if some are too large. Have any particularly large groups divide in half, for example. As a group, they should discuss the following questions:

- What are key components of this stage?
- What challenges have you observed due to being in this stage?
- What victories have you experienced or do you hope to experience in this stage?
- What strategies might you see to assist the members of this group to proceed to the next stage?
  Allow 15 minutes.

Invite the students to develop a creative way to demonstrate this stage of group development. They could act out a scene to demonstrate this stage, develop a commercial to "sell" the stage, or change the words of a popular song to describe the stage.

After each group's presentation, facilitate a discussion about the important elements described in the text.

Allow 15 minutes.

Variation   If this session is a part of a cohort experience or course, you could use this activity as a small group assignment.

Activity 2: Adjourning and the Role of a Leader

Time: 25 minutes

The adjourning stage of group development can easily get overlooked especially with groups who have a fixed term.

Student organizations are a perfect example of such groups, as in most scenarios they have high turnover in officers from year to year. When the student organization completes a large event or experience, they select new officers and begin the group development process all over again. Unfortunately, missing that time at the end of the experience to thoughtfully move through the adjourning stage is a place many organizations find themselves.

Scenario   You are a member of a service organization that contributes 10,000 hours of service per year as an organization to local nonprofits in College Town, USA. Each year they select new officers in April, which leaves little time for them to transition. They have never fully moved through the adjourning stage of group development as an executive team or organization.

Divide students in small discussion groups and ask them to develop a comprehensive plan that would help this organization move through the adjourning stage. Allow 10 minutes.

1. How can members take time to pause and make meaning of the experience they have had together?
2. How can members be recognized?
3. How can the executive team explore what they have learned over the course of the year?
4. What other stakeholders should be involved in this stage?
5. How will they celebrate their success?

Once the students have developed a plan, invite them to share their plans to the entire class. Allow 20 minutes.

Activity Variation   If you have access to resources on Love Languages, this could be an informative and fun assessment that the students could take to reflect on how they like to receive recognition. You can connect this knowledge base to what the adjourning phase could look like in a student organization.

> Facilitator Notes

When facilitating conversations related to Tuckman's model, it is helpful to allow students to guide the conversation and identify their own experiences to help the model come to life. Facilitators should touch base with each group to encourage them to explore further questions.

Melissa Shehane serves as the program coordinator for the Leadership and Service Center at Texas A&M University. Melissa coordinates community engagement efforts within her department, as well as service-learning opportunities with faculty and other stakeholders. Her primary focus is to develop civically minded leaders. She earned a master's degree in college student affairs from The Pennsylvania State University in May 2007 and is pursuing a PhD in agricultural leadership, education, and communications at Texas A&M University.

Active Learning Module 8b

Group Dynamics and Group Roles

Eric Kaufman

> Summary of Concepts

This learning module addresses a portion of Chapter 8, Interacting in Teams and Groups. In this section, students explore group dynamics, including group roles and group norms.

Groups engage in various processes that are often called group dynamics. Group dynamics include such processes as how the group makes decisions, how the group handles its conflict, and how the group meets its leadership needs. Group roles and group norms are the driving influences of group dynamics.

Groups depend on two kinds of roles: group-building roles and task roles. Group-building roles are actions that focus on the group as people, including the relationships among members. Task roles focus on accomplishing the purposes of the group, including giving information and opinions and moving the group along on tasks by summarizing and using various decision-making strategies.

Group norms are the rules of conduct that lead to consistent practices in a group. Some norms are explicit and clearly seen by all participants. Other norms may have evolved through the cultural practices of the group. The group norms collectively contribute to the group's overall personality.

> Learning Outcomes

Students will

- Apply both group-building roles and task roles in a group activity
- Consider how group norms impact the functioning of teams and groups
- Be able to articulate group norms for a specific organization

> Module Overview

Lead students in an activity called "balloon challenge," which provides the opportunity to engage in both group-building roles and task roles. Through several iterations of the activity, students will be able to experiment with and alternate between different roles. This is followed by small group discussions about the development of group norms, reflecting on both the balloon challenge and students' personal experiences. Finally, students are invited to articulate group norms for a specific organization in the form of hieroglyphics (i.e., cave-type drawings).

Estimated Time

Activity 1: Balloon Challenge, 20-minute activity, 10-minute discussion

Activity 2: Experience with Group Norms, 5-minute small group discussion, 10-minute large group sharing

Activity 3: Hieroglyphic Moment, 10-minute small group work, 5-minute large group sharing

Materials/Supplies

Packages of multicolored balloons (one balloon per student plus one balloon per group)

Permanent markers (at least one per group) to write on balloons

Flip chart paper (or alternate medium) to capture ideas from large and small groups

> Module Activities

Activity 1: Balloon Challenge

Time: 30 minutes

Explain to students that this activity allows them to experience and practice key components of group dynamics.

Divide students into groups of four to seven people. Give each person a different colored balloon (ensuring a variety of colors within each group). Ask them to blow up and tie their balloon. Then ask them to write their name on the balloon with a permanent marker. (Note: Nonpermanent markers may smear.) Explain that they will be responsible for not letting their own balloon touch the ground.

Then give each group an extra balloon of another color (e.g., red) and tell them that this is the "team balloon." Explain that it belongs to no one in particular but is the responsibility of the entire team. Tell them that they must keep the balloons afloat for two minutes and that the team will be awarded points for each balloon they keep afloat. Indicate that different color balloons are worth different points. For example:

Yellow = 1 point

Green = 3 points

Blue = 5 points

Pink = 7 points

Red (the team balloon) = 15 points

Tell them to begin. After a period of time, increase the difficulty by not allowing them to use their hands or by specifying the body part that they must use (knees, feet, etc.). After two minutes call time and total the group scores based on which balloons they kept afloat.

Ask each group to develop a strategy for improving their performance. (If any groups achieved all of the points possible, encourage them to propose criteria for bonus points.) After about two minutes of group discussion on appropriate strategies, begin the two-minute balloon challenge again.

Following the second round of the balloon challenge, ask the groups to share among their members how they feel about their performance with the activity. Encourage them to develop a strategy for ensuring all members of the group remain included and enjoy the activity. After about two minutes of group discussion on appropriate strategies, begin the two-minute balloon challenge again.

Debriefing Questions

- How did this activity reveal group dynamics?
  - How did your group handle the "team balloon"?
  - Did it matter that each of you had your name on a particular balloon? Explain.
- Following the first round of the balloon challenge, when you had the opportunity to discuss a strategy, what group roles were highlighted in the discussion?
  - Was the discussion more about group-building (i.e., maintaining positive relationships) or task roles?
  - What (if any) dysfunctional roles hampered the group's progress?
- How did the discussion and strategy change between rounds two and three?
  - What group-building strategies did you employ?
  - Did you default to a particular role set (i.e., preferred set of practices)?

- How do different combinations of group roles contribute to group norms?
  - Was there a different culture or personality among certain groups? Why?
  - What group norms would be best suited for success with this activity?

Variation   After the second round of the balloon challenge, partner high-performing groups with low-performing groups, encouraging the high performers to coach and encourage the low performers.

Activity 2: Experience with Group Norms

Time: 15 minutes

In pairs or small groups, have students identify at least one organization with which they are familiar. Ask them to consider the following:

- How would you describe the personality of the organization?
  - Is it more relationship- or task-oriented?
  - Are there multiple level and layers of leadership, or is it a more open structure?
- How does the organization articulate rules of conduct?
  - Does it have bylaws or published meeting procedures?
  - Is there an orientation for new members?
- For group norms that are not clearly articulated, how do members know about them?
  - How are guests or new members introduced to the organization?
  - What cues for accepted behavior are visible at organizational meetings?

Ask each group to share their experiences with the larger group. Compare and contrast different organizations. Engage the group in a discussion about the issues raised. As students share, connect their statements back to the readings. Ask them to consider how group norms influence group roles (i.e., group-building roles and task roles). Ask them to consider how the opposite is also true.

Activity 3: Hieroglyphic Moment

Time: 15 minutes

Ask students to return to their small groups and articulate the chosen organization's norms in the form of hieroglyphics (i.e., cave-type drawings). Encourage them to think of these hieroglyphics like road signs, directing new members how to proceed and what to watch for. To the degree possible, encourage competition between groups, offering extra recognition to the group with the most instructive or creative hieroglyphics. After each group has had sufficient time to prepare their hieroglyphics, invite them to share their drawings with the larger group.

> Facilitator Notes

The balloon challenge is adapted from an activity in the *Instructor's Manual for Mastering Self-Leadership* (6th edition) (2013). The hieroglyphic activity is adapted from *Strategies for Great Teaching* (2004).

If latex balloons are used, students with latex allergies will not be able to fully participate in the balloon challenge. However, having the group remain responsible for that individual's balloon can help surface discussions about diversity and what to do about individual limitations.

The balloon challenge is likely to surface many issues related to groups and teams. The discussion will probably include stages of group development as well as goal setting. Be prepared for a broader discussion than the focus readings.

When students share examples from their own experience, be sure to balance stories of group dysfunction with positive stories of group success.

> References

Houghton, J. D., & Lewis-Brim, C. F. (2013). *Instructor's manual for mastering self-leadership* (6th ed) Upper Saddle River, NJ: Pearson/Prentice Hall.

Reardon M., & Derner, S. (2004). *Strategies for great teaching: Maximize learning moments.* Saint Paul, MN: Zephyr Press.

Eric Kaufman is an assistant professor of leadership in the Department of Agricultural and Extension Education at Virginia Tech University. In this role, he coordinates the university's graduate certificate in Collaborative Community Leadership and supports the undergraduate minor in leadership and social change.

Active Learning Module 8c

Creative Conflict in Groups

Daniel Tillapaugh

> Summary of Concepts

This learning module addresses a portion of Chapter 8, Interacting in Teams and Groups. In this section, students explore creative conflict. While many students prefer to avoid it, when handled skillfully, conflict can serve groups well. Conflict helps groups clarify values and arrive at better, more creative solutions. Within this section, students learn three conflict resolution outcomes; these include (1) win-win, (2) win-lose, and (3) lose-lose. Viewing these outcomes using the lens of the Relational Leadership Model, a win-win outcome typically results from healthy collaboration and communication between all parties, whereas win-lose and lose-lose outcomes always result in someone or a group of people feeling marginalized and excluded. Strategies for working through conflict and encouraging a break from "groupthink" are provided to have students consider how to work through their group's conflicts aiming towards a win-win outcome.

> Learning Outcomes

Students will

- Understand how different types of conflict arise in groups
- Identify the distinctions between win-win, win-lose, and lose-lose conflict resolution outcomes
- Consider several strategies to handle group conflicts effectively

> Module Overview

Students engage in a self-reflection exercise using paper and markers to draw how they typically feel when dealing with conflict. In small groups, the students take turns sharing their pieces and having their peers share what insights they can make from the drawings, followed by discussion as a large group. Students then learn about the Behavior-Feelings-Reason model of discussing conflict and apply it into action in a group role-play activity.

Estimated Time
Activity 1: Drawing Conflict, 20 minutes
Activity 2: Behavior-Feelings-Reason Think-Pair-Share,
     10 minutes
Activity 3: Conflict in Action Role-Play and Reflection,
     30 minutes

Materials/Supplies
Newsprint
Markers
Board or flip chart to write down points from discussion
Conflict scenarios on small strips of paper
Bowl or hat for conflict scenarios
Copies of the scenario for role-play and short "role" descriptions
     to assign to students

> Module Activities

Activity 1: Drawing Conflict

Time: 20 minutes

Explain to students this activity is meant to have them reflect upon their experiences in dealing with conflicts that arise when involved in a group (i.e., sports team, student organization, group project).

Each student should take a piece of newsprint and some markers and draw an interpretation of what that conflict felt like for them. They should consider what their natural inclination was in how to manage that conflict and make sure that they represent that pictorially.

After five minutes, organize students into groups of two or three to share their drawings. Rather than telling their peers about their drawing, they should invite them to provide their perspectives about what they see in the drawing. After everyone else has made some remarks about what they saw in the picture, the student who drew it explains what he or she drew and also comment on the insights gleaned from the feedback given. Each group should spend two to three minutes discussing everyone's drawings. The facilitator can use the debriefing questions below for the whole group to process the activity.

Debriefing Questions

* What is your natural instinct for dealing with conflict within a group?
* When you were drawing your experience with conflict, how easily did you get brought back into that experience? How do you think that specific experience might play into similar experiences in the future?
* What was experience like of listening to other people interpret your drawing of your conflict situation?

- Were there any insights gained from your peers around your drawing that may have informed some further thinking around conflict for you?

Variation Instead of having students draw their own images, the facilitator could set out photo cards (random photographs with a wide array of images that might conjure up different emotions or feelings preferably) or use Visual Explorer cards (available for purchase through the Center for Creative Leadership). Ask students to review the images while reflecting upon a specific instance of dealing with conflict in a group, and choose an image.

Activity 2: Behavior-Feelings-Reason

Time: 10 minutes

To frame this activity, the facilitator should provide a brief (two minutes or less) overview of the Behavior-Feelings-Reason model of dealing with conflict, seen below. It may be helpful to write the following on a board or have it on newsprint hung in the room:

"When you (name the behavior), I feel (state the feeling or emotion) because (provide the reason)."

As a means of having students practice this, pair them up with a partner and have each student draw a small slip of paper out of a bowl or hat with different conflict-filled scenarios (see Conflict Scenarios at the end of the module). Students should use the Behavior-Feelings-Reason model with their partner based upon their chosen scenario. Each should take turns practicing this model of addressing conflict.

Discuss connections to the *Exploring Leadership* reading:

- How might the Behavior-Feelings-Reason model assist you in negotiating conflict in groups or organizations?
- How do our reactions to conflict through the language we use make an impact on the situation?

- Think back to the concepts of lose-lose, win-lose, or win-win situations discussed in the chapter. Can you think of examples where situations became lose-lose or win-lose due to the language people used in their work with another? How about examples of win-win situations? What were the differences between the two?

Variation   Instead of providing students with conflict scenarios, have them think back to their conflict in Activity One. Have them reflect upon the situation they were recalling then and use Behavior-Feeling-Reason model in their statements to their partners.

Activity 3: Conflict in Action

Time: 30 minutes

Students participate in a role-play activity that simulates conflict in organizations and groups. The facilitator may use the scenario and "roles" provided or feel free to adapt this example to another scenario that may best fit the students' experiences.

The facilitator distributes an envelope to each student, which includes a copy of the scenario as well as his or her assigned role and pertinent information related to the role. Tell the students they have two minutes to review the information inside their envelope carefully and then at the end of that two minute period, the student who has been assigned the "chair" role should convene the group and begin working to address the task outlined in the role play's scenario.

Give the students 15 minutes once the chair begins the group's work to play out the scenario. During the activity give them occasional time warnings (especially when they have five minutes and one minute remaining). Once time is up, debrief the activity.

Debriefing Questions

- What was it like playing a role that may have been unfamiliar to you?
- How did you feel as the role-play went on, particularly if the conflict increased at times? What caused you to feel the way that you did?
- What group dynamics did you observe that created conflict for the group?
- How might personal agendas or hidden agendas create further issues for the group? What would you do about this had this been a real situation in a group in which you were a member?
- How might the group have worked together to create this scenario to be a win-win? What strategies may have been important to use for that to have been the outcome?
- How did people in the group utilize Behavior-Feelings-Reason statements? How might they have? Would it have helped the group's process?

> Facilitator Notes

Conflicts in groups and organizations often bring up a whole host of reflections and emotions from students. More often than not, students very easily can think of a difficult conflict in which they were a part, whether it was a personal conflict or one in a group setting. These experiences also usually generate quite a bit of discussion and storytelling, so it will be important to plan for students to want to discuss their personal experiences. You may want to encourage them to connect their experiences directly to the ideas discussed in the reading to help them synthesize material and connect concepts effectively.

> Conflict Scenarios

For this activity, have each of the following scenarios on separate strips of paper in a hat or bowl for students to pick at random. There are several examples that you could use. However, feel free to brainstorm other scenarios, especially ones that may be applicable to students within your group. The more "real" the scenarios, the more effective the overall practice of this activity will be.

Your roommate has been watching the television or listening to music very loudly at night when you would like to be sleeping causing some frustration lately.

You loaned your friend some money a month ago to pay off some of their bills and she or he has not paid you back yet.

You overheard your friend talking badly about you recently to another friend.

Your teammate has been really negative about the team's string of losses lately, and it has started to affect the team's morale.

Your group member is not following through on their obligations as well as not meeting the group's imposed deadlines.

A member of your student organization has a personal issue with another member of your team and that is having an impact on the group's overall effectiveness.

These are several examples that you could use. However, feel free to brainstorm other scenarios, especially ones that may be applicable to students within your group. The more "real" the scenarios, the more effective the overall practice of this activity will be.

> Role Play Scenario and Roles

Scenario

Each of the students should be provided a copy of the scenario.

The dean of students has called you to an emergency meeting with other student leaders on campus. Upon arrival, the dean tells the group that an anonymous donor has given the institution a gift of $750,000 to be designated for either the expansion of the campus's student union building or the creation of a new scholarship program geared toward economically disadvantaged applicants. The condition of the gift is that it is up to a specific group of student leaders identified by the donor to work together to make the final decision of which project gets funded, and the group must reach consensus within 15 minutes.

The dean will return in 15 minutes to learn of the final decision of the group. At this point, the student who has been designated as chair should begin the group's decision-making process.

Roles

Each of the students should be assigned one of the following roles. Roles designed with an asterisk (*) could be assigned to multiple students, depending upon the size of your group.

Chair   You are the designated chair for this meeting. Selected personally by the anonymous donor, your goal is to use the 15 minutes wisely, keeping everyone on track and focused to reach a decision with which everyone can agree. Remember: everyone must agree on one of these projects to fund by the time limit or neither project will be funded. Be aware of factions and personal agendas that may arise.

President, Multicultural Student Union   As president of the Multicultural Student Union, you feel strongly that the funds should be put toward the establishment of scholarships for economically disadvantaged students. These funds would be important for continuing to provide access for students who typically could not afford attending college. From your perspective, that is more important than adding more space to the student center which was renovated ten years ago. Do everything you can to promote your peers to vote for the scholarship funds.

Resident Assistant*   You have been a resident assistant on campus the past two years, and you recognize that both projects could be really useful for this institution. Vote your conscience and what you think is right based upon the points that the group brings up.

Orientation Leader*   You have been an orientation leader on campus the past three years, and you recognize that both projects could be really useful for this institution. Vote your conscience and what you think is right based upon the points that the group brings up.

Student Employee, Student Union*   As a student worker in the Student Union, you are quite aware that space is at a premium within the building. A huge increase in the number of student organizations on campus the past four years has resulted in lots of traffic within the Union during almost all of the building's operating hours. This money could be really helpful in providing additional meeting room and office space—not to mention a much needed coffeehouse and performing arts space in the building. You know that the scholarship money could also be useful, but your allegiance is with the Student Union. Try to convince others to see your point of view and vote for that project.

Upward Bound Head Counselor   As the head counselor of the Upward Bound program, you know that many of the students you've been working with in Upward Bound would benefit from the scholarship funds. However, you're also aware that if the Student Union expansion happened, the Upward Bound program would finally be able to move their offices into this new space. After being moved around from building to building over the past five years, often in spaces that were far away from student traffic, it'd be terrific to have a permanent home at the heart of campus. You're torn, and you'll need to listen to the arguments of others to figure out just where exactly you want to vote.

Captain, Women's Track and Field   As Captain of the Women's Track and Field team, you find it ridiculous that you have to vote for either of these two projects. The money, in your opinion, should really be spent on building a much-needed indoor track arena that could also be used as a multipurpose venue for the campus. The campus could attract big name entertainers and audiences, generating more money for the institution, and your team could have a year-round, top-quality space for practices and meets. You should do everything you can to convince everyone to join your line of thinking. However, in the end, if you can't convince everyone to join your view, support the vote of your best friend, the Upward Bound Head Counselor.

Student Government School of Business Senator   You and the chair have never gotten along, and your personal issues with the chair still are unresolved. You believe that you should be running this meeting, and you feel as though the chair should know that you're unhappy and that you would be the better choice to lead these proceedings. Ultimately though, you're going to do anything to support your best friend, the president of the Multicultural Student Union.

Daniel Tillapaugh is the Postdoctoral Fellow in Higher Education at the University of Maine. He earned his PhD at the University of San Diego's Leadership Studies program where he taught in the undergraduate leadership studies minor.

Active Learning Module 8d

Group Decision Making

Daniel Ostick

> Summary of Concepts

This learning module addresses a portion of Chapter 8, Interacting in Teams and Groups. In this section, students explore group decision making. While decision making is not always a group process, group leaders should consider if decisions support the group's vision and mission, what opinions group members have about the issue, whether the decision will heighten or limit involvement, if the decision is ethical and principled, and if he or she should slow down making the decision so that others can get involved.

The empowerment and commitment of group members is enhanced through a good group decision-making process. Group members should be and have a right to be involved in key decisions. Decision-making processes vary in degrees of leader control, the value of input, and the importance of individual buy-in. Consensus models of decision making, while time consuming, offer opportunities for individual empowerment and increase the possibility of group buy-in. Comfort with conflict, active listening skills, and mutual respect are necessary skills for successful consensus building.

> Learning Outcomes

Students will

- Understand the pros and cons of different approaches to group decision making
- Apply the consensus model of group decision making

> Module Overview

Students explore the pros and cons of a variety of decision-making methods in small groups. They then engage in a consensus-building activity that allows them to practice a powerful but challenging approach to group decision making.

Estimated Time
Activity 1: Group Decision-Making Approaches, 25 minutes
Activity 2: Consensus Building, 30 minutes

Materials/Supplies
No materials necessary for activities

> Module Activities

Activity 1: Group Decision-Making Approaches

Time: 25 minutes

    Exploring Leadership briefly outlines Johnson and Johnson's (2006) seven methods of decision making, as follows: (1) decision by authority without discussion, (2) expert member, (3) average members' opinions, (4) decision by authority after discussion, (5) minority control, (6) majority control, and (7) consensus.

Divide the large group into six smaller groups, one group for each model (excluding consensus). Have each group answer four questions:

- What does this method mean? (You may provide if it is unclear.)
- What are the strengths of this approach?
- What are the weaknesses of this approach?
- When and why have you used this approach?

After each group works through their answers (approximately 10 minutes), have them report out to the class and facilitate a conversation to bring forth additional ideas and make connections (approximately 15 minutes). A critical area to explore will be to ask what the impact was when their approach did not work in real life and how they approached it differently after that.

If needed, here are some brief definitions of each method and strengths and weaknesses. Do not share the strengths and weaknesses prior to the activity. Instead, use them to further the discussion. This list of definitions and critiques were adapted from the Foundation Coalition (www.foundationcoalition.org).

Method 1. Decision by Authority Without Discussion

Process—The designated leader makes all decisions without consulting group members.

Strengths—Takes minimal time to make decision; commonly used in organizations (so we are familiar with method); high on assertiveness

Weaknesses—No group interaction; team may not understand decision or be unable to implement decision; low on cooperation

Appropriate Times for Method 1—Simple, routine, administrative decisions; little time available to make decision; team commitment required to implement the decision is low

Method 2. Decision by Expert Member

Process—Select the expert from group, let the expert consider the issues, and let the expert make decisions.

Strengths—Useful when one person on the team has the overwhelming expertise

Weaknesses—Unclear how to determine who the expert is (team members may have different opinions); no group interaction; may become popularity issue or power issue

Appropriate Times for Method 2—Result is highly dependent on specific expertise, clear choice for expert, team commitment required to implement decision is low

Method 3. Average Members' Opinions

Process—Separately ask each team member his or her opinion and average the results

Strengths—Extreme opinions cancelled out; error typically cancelled out; group members consulted; useful when it is difficult to get the team together to talk; urgent decisions can be made

Weaknesses—No group interaction, team members are not truly involved in the decision; opinions of least and most knowledgeable members may cancel; commitment to decision may not be strong; unresolved conflict may exist or escalate; may damage future team effectiveness

Appropriate Times for Method 3—Time available for decision is limited; team participation is required, but lengthy interaction is undesirable; team commitment required to implement the decision is low

Method 4. Decision by Authority after Discussion

Process—The team creates ideas and has discussions, but the designated leader makes the final decision. The designated leader calls a meeting, presents the issue, listens to discussion from the team, and announces her or his decision.

Strengths—Team used more than methods 1–3; listening to the team increases the accuracy of the decision

Weaknesses—Team is not part of decision; team may compete for the leader's attention; team members may tell leader "what he or she wants to hear"; still may not have commitment from the team to the decision

Appropriate Times for Method 4—Available time allows team interaction but not agreement; clear consensus on authority; team commitment required to implement decision is moderately low

Method 5. Minority Control

Process—A minority of the team, two or more members who constitute less than 50% of the team, make the team's decision

Strengths—Method often used by executive committees; method can be used by temporary committees; useful for large number of decisions and limited time; some team perspective and discussion

Weaknesses—Can be railroading; may not have full team commitment to decision; may create an air of competition among team members; still may not have commitment from team to decision

Appropriate Times for Method 5—Limited time prevents convening entire team; clear choice of minority group; team commitment required to implement the decision is moderately low

Method 6. Majority Control

Process—This is the most commonly used method in the United States (not synonymous with best method). Discuss the decision until 51% or more of the team members make the decision.

Strengths—Useful when there is insufficient time to make decision by consensus; useful when complete team-member commitment is unnecessary for implementing a decision

Weaknesses—Taken for granted as the natural, or only, way for teams to make a decision; team is viewed as the "winners and the losers"; reduces the quality of decision; minority opinion not discussed and may not be valued; may have unresolved and unaddressed conflict; full group interaction is not obtained

Appropriate Times for Method 6—Time constraints require decision; group consensus supporting voting process; team commitment required to implement decision is moderately high

Activity 2: Consensus Building

Time: 30 minutes

With the entire group, review the definition and pros and cons of using a consensus approach to group decision making.

Definition of consensus (from text) Rayner (1996): "Consensus does not mean that everyone on the team thinks the best possible decision has been reached. It does mean that no one is professionally violated by the decision and that all team members will support its implementation." The process involves a fair communication process where everyone speaks and listens and all are valued and feel understood. Consensus does take more time and takes a lot of energy and commitment from group members. Consensus means everyone can live with the final decision.

Ask for five to six volunteers from the large group and ask them to form a circle in the middle of the room. The remainder of the students will be on the outside observing the process and taking notes on the process.

Inform the small group that they will be using consensus to make a group decision. Before posing the question or issue, ask the large group if they have any tips or words of advice for coming to consensus. Write these tips on the board as an active reminder of good practices. Items to include might be

- Clearly define the issue
- Focus on similarities between positions

- Don't rush the process
- Avoid voting
- Use active listening and try to compromise
- Encouraging all points of view and allow people to disagree with each other with civility
- Regularly check in to ensure group agreement

The question or issue can be generated by the class, but should be a topic that has high commitment and interest and a variety of opinions. If you are working with an intact group of students from a student organization, you may want to pose a question related to their mission (i.e., what fundraising program should the group develop for this year?). Two possible topics that will likely generate discussion for any group of students are as follows:

- How should campus improve parking policies for students?
- How should campus distribute athletic tickets to students?

Give the group ample time to attempt to come to consensus. This may take up to 15 minutes, but you may need to cut off discussion before consensus is reached if time is limited.

When time is up or the group is finished, facilitate a conversation (15 minutes) about the process, asking questions of the small group and the large group:

- Was this process challenging or easy? How so?
- Which of the tips did you actively use? Which were harder to engage with?
- What did the group do that was helpful to the process? (for the large group)
- What could the group have done differently to improve? (for the large group)
- Would another one of the decision making methods been more appropriate? Why?
- When have you used consensus in your own groups and organizations? What were the payoffs or costs?

> Facilitator Notes

A challenge in engaging in active consensus building for a group of students is that the level of active interest and commitment to the topic and the decision being made is likely to be low. For consensus to be a more appropriate method of decision making than other methods, the commitment must be high, so identifying a good topic is crucial. A simple topic will result in a very fast process because students may not be invested in the outcome and a too challenging topic may result in gridlock or hurt feelings.

Consider giving the group an actual decision to make, if appropriate. For an academic class, can they decide what the final presentation for the class will be or what the format of the final exam will be? For a student organization, can they decide what the election process for the following year will be? If so, consider engaging the whole class in the consensus building activity. Otherwise, it would be a "minority control" method.

> References

Johnson, D. W., & Johnson, F. P. (2006). *Joining together: Group theory and group skills* (9th ed). Boston, MA: Allyn & Bacon.

Rayner, S. R. (1996). *Team traps: Survival stories and lessons from team disasters, near-misses, mishaps, and other near-death experiences.* New York, NY: Wiley

Daniel T. Ostick serves as the coordinator for leadership curriculum development and academic partnerships in the Adele H. Stamp Student Union–Center for Campus Life at the University of Maryland. He earned a PhD in college student personnel from the University of Maryland.

Active Learning Module 8e

Roles in Teams and Groups

Meredith A. Smith, Tyler L. McClain

> Summary of Concepts

This learning module addresses Chapter 8, Interacting in Teams and Groups. Critical for understanding group dynamics is to understand the variety of roles group members fill. Recognizing the ways in which group members communicate their roles to each other is an important skill for fostering a good group process and effective group dynamics. Groups depend on two kinds of roles: group-building roles and task roles.

> Learning Outcomes

Students will

- Be able to identify the complex roles that exist within groups and teams and relate the roles to their own involvement experiences

- Apply learned knowledge of the Relational Leadership Model to group and team process and build their own leadership self-efficacy toward working with others
- Utilize Relational Leadership Model strategies to become effective group and team leaders regardless of position or role

> Module Overview

Students participate in a simulation activity involving typical roles that exist within groups. Students will be assigned a specific role to demonstrate. Modifications are listed for groups of varying sizes. Following the activity, students will debrief the simulation and will be given the opportunity to reflect on the roles they typically perform in group settings. The discussion should culminate in students thinking critically about implications for their future practice.

In small groups students will analyze group process case studies based upon examples listed in Chapter 8. Students will be provided with toolkit action cards with strategies that fit well within the Relational Leadership Model. Using the toolkit cards, students will examine the group process and make recommendations. Moreover, students will apply the toolkit strategies to their own past and present group experiences.

Estimated Time
Activity 1: Group Roles and Observations, 40 minutes
- Discussion Simulation: 15 Minutes
- Group Discussion: 20 Minutes
- Future Implications: 5 Minutes
Activity 2: Team Action Toolkit, 20 minutes
- Toolkit Activity: 10 Minutes
- Discussion: 10 Minutes

Material/Supplies

Blank paper and pens/pencils

A set of index cards with a group role and description written on each (provided below)

A set of team action toolkit cards for each small group (description provided below)

Markers

› Module Activities

Activity 1: Group Roles & Observations

Time: 40 minutes

This activity provides an understanding of the typical group roles that affect group dynamics and process. Students should be seated in a circle so that everyone can see each other. Have each student select one card from the set of group roles cards. If the group contains more than seven individuals, group roles can be repeated or groups may be subdivided into groups of appropriate size at the facilitator's discretion (*see activity variations for more information*). Students should not share their role with the group until after the simulation is completed. After the roles have been determined, select one scenario and provide a 15-minute time limit for discussion. It is useful to provide 5-minute and 1-minute time warnings.

Group Roles (for index cards)

- Group Maintenance

  Focused on group dynamics especially the relationships demonstrated among group members. This role focuses on the needs of other group members and is attentive to creating harmony among them.

- Task
  Focused on accomplishing the purpose of the group, including giving information and opinions and moving the group along by summarizing and by using various decision-making strategies. This role is focused on completing the scenario efficiently and within the allotted time frame.
- Special Interest Pleader
  Focused on pushing their point like a broken record. People in this role try to prevent the group from moving on when they are not getting their way.
- Blocker
  Focused on resisting or blocking any group action by being negative and disagreeable about everything. Feel free to use phrases such as "this is unproductive" or "I don't agree with that statement."
- Active Member
  Focused on being actively engaged through listening and supporting the group decision-making process. This role should speak when something important needs to be stated but should not dominate the discussion.
- Nonparticipant
  Focused on other things outside of what the group is working on and does not even listen or engage other members of the group in anyway. This role may text, update social media status to "most boring meeting ever," and mumble verbally "I don't know why I'm here."
- Observer
  Focused on recording the interactions between the group members. This role should try to identify the other roles in the group. Observer should not speak unless spoken to directly.

Scenarios
- Your organization is planning to bring a speaker to campus who exemplifies the values of your organization such as integrity

and hard work. You've narrowed the invite list down to two speakers in your organization's price range. Speaker one is a notable TV personality best identified with their exploits on a popular reality show. Speaker two is a retired news anchor with a long résumé of awards for journalistic integrity.

- You are on an executive board for a large student group on-campus. Your group has struggled to get general members to attend group meetings. Your next general meeting is critical because if you loose any more involved members, your group may no longer be eligible for funding through your university's club requirements.

- Your student group is reevaluating its marketing strategies for the coming semester due to lack of attendance at programs and meetings. General members have expressed concerns about the amount of paper used on-campus and their lack of attention to the over abundance of email and social media messages.

- Your group is attempting to plan its first ever service project. There are three local nonprofit organizations that are interested in hosting your group. Nonprofit one organizes local park cleanup and beautification projects for Saturday mornings. Nonprofit two is a local soup kitchen that serves dinner at 8 P.M. on Friday nights. Nonprofit three is an afterschool tutoring program that requires volunteers to be paired with a few local elementary school students and work with those students for an entire quarter.

Debriefing Questions
- Was the group successful at accomplishing the given task? Why or why not?
- Describe your experience demonstrating these roles.
- What role would you have liked to demonstrate in this simulation and why?
- What role do you actually perform in group meetings? Does this role change depending on the group?

- Together the students should share their prior knowledge about how they have experienced these roles in past or current groups. Student should discuss how they can better understand and work with individuals who display characteristics of these roles.
- Observers—what actions or statements helped the discussion move forward?
- Observers—what actions or statements hindered group progress?
- As a group discuss what strategies are best for encountering each role.
- If time allows, provide the students with paper to write down their own thoughts or feelings related to the simulation using these guiding questions. Then discuss the key implications as a group. If time is running short the facilitator may choose to skip the written reflection portion and pose these questions directly to the group.
  - What surprised you about this exercise?
  - Do you have any lingering questions or concerns (fears) when working with others?
  - What new knowledge or concepts have you gained from this activity?

Variations   The facilitator may also choose to take on the observer role. This is especially beneficial if they are in an advising role with the students participating in this activity.

If the student group is smaller than seven students, one may opt to select only certain roles for students to simulate or choose to provide each student multiple roles. Here are some suggested pairings for multiple roles:

- Group Maintenance/Active Member
- Task/Special Interest Pleader

- Nonparticipant/Observer
- Blocker is recommended as a stand alone role. The blocker still participates, although it may be perceived in a negative way.

The scenarios listed are generic so that students can relate the situations to their own experience. Feel free to modify or add one's own scenarios to specific groups or teams that they find their students are involved in. If time allows, multiple scenarios can be facilitated prior to the debriefing discussion.

Activity 2: Team Action Toolkit

Time: 20 minutes

This activity will provide students with experience in applying the Relational Leadership Model to case studies based upon examples in the chapter. To prepare for this activity, assemble a toolkit index card packet for each small group. Print each "tool" listed below (see toolkit cards) on its own index card.

Divide students into groups of three to four. Each group will receive a case study and a set of toolkit cards. Students should use the toolkit to explain the key implications of the case study as it pertains to group and team process.

Toolkit Cards

- *Creative Conflict* includes setting ground rules for group discussions, disagreeing with civility and ensuring that everyone's voice is heard.
- *Group Decision Making* puts emphasis on mission/vision based decisions, checking in with group members to hear opinions, understanding who should be involved in the decision making process and how they should be involved. Additionally decisions should be ethical, and should be made knowing the group's expectations in the decision making process.

- *Teams and Teamwork* relates to group morale, motivation, support of each other, common purpose, diversity of roles, inclusion of others, sense of group identity and interdependence of group members.
- *Goal Setting* is all about establishing group trust, and creating SMART goals (Specific Measurable Attainable Relevant Time-bound goals).
- *Team Learning* occurs through dialogue of personal experiences, values and stories, as well as collective listening, reflection, and thought.
- *Individual Leadership* involves serving as a facilitator for team learning. One must reflect on their own personal motivations, advocate for others, and reflect on group process and outcomes.
- *Team Leadership* consists of team members feeling valued, teams that are effective in achieving the goals they set out to accomplish, and a careful balance between monitoring, taking action, and paying attention.
- Create Your Own: A tool or item not here, create your own (e.g. Ask your advisor).

Case-Studies Based upon the Chapter

- **Students in STEM** had a very concerning last meeting with only three members present. They are a month away from what is supposed to be a large celebration in honor of their 100th anniversary as an organization. Early on in the semester, there was a lot of excitement and group energy toward the celebration. The group leader led several brainstorming sessions until consensus was reach that the celebration should be a campus-wide concert. In the next meeting however, the group was informed that a concert would be logistically out of their budget range and was asked to brainstorm again what type of celebration should take place. At this point, many members were confused and began to question their purpose in being at the meeting and the purpose of the organization.

- The **Business Entrepreneurs Club (BEC)** is locked in a fierce debate over what activities the organization should engage in. Robert is a new member at his first meeting. He notices that the group meeting consists of one continuous argument in which members are debating whether to design a logo for boxer shorts and use the profits to host a party or design a T-Shirt to raise money for a local recreational charity. The group meeting seems incredibly divided with two subgroups competing for attention and ultimately the final say on what activities the BEC should engage in. Robert is unsure of whether he will show up for another meeting.

- The **Black Student Union (BSU)**, a once strong organization on campus recently decided to vote itself out of existence due to dwindling attendance at social events and lack of interest. Several members of the group met up and reformed a new group called Umoja (meaning Unity) with a new purpose aimed at being inclusive of all students on campus, and providing wide ranged events including social, educational, and advocacy events for campus. Recently, the Umoja leadership team was approached by a group of BSU alumni donors wondering why BSU was no longer in existence. Umoja is currently crafting a response to the alumni group.

Students should briefly present on how they analyzed the case study.

Debrief Questions
Scenario-Specific Questions
- Students in STEM: Using your toolkit, what opportunities for group development were missed during the past several meetings of students in STEM? If you were a member of this organization what would you have done differently? If

you were a student in this group, how would you utilize the toolkit after only three members attended your last meeting?

- BEC: Using your toolkit, what tools would be helpful for BEC to reach some sort of consensus? If you are Robert, at your first meeting, what are your initial reactions to the espoused mission of the group and the actual actions of the group?
- BSU/Umoja: Using the toolkit, why do you think BSU took a bold step of disassembling? What tools did the new Umoja demonstrate in their actions and what would be a good response to the BSU alumni group?

General Questions

- What success or failure experiences have you witnesses as a member of a group?
  - How did you address those experiences?
  - What toolkit items would have been helpful at the time?

Variations   Students may also want to brainstorm problems they are facing in current groups and organizations and then utilize their toolkit to solve the problem or analyze it. You may also want to use non-chapter examples for the case-study exercise:

- Student generated scenarios
- Your group has decided to plan a charity walk on campus, what items from the toolkit will you need and how will you use each item to achieve this task.
- Your group has recently been losing members, what items from the toolkit will you need and how will you use each item to take corrective actions.

Prior to analyzing scenarios, provide each student group with six blank sticky notes or index cards to create their own toolkit utilizing knowledge from their own experience and the chapter reading. The student generated toolkit can be related directly back to the chapter through the debrief portion of the activity.

> Facilitator's Notes

The module authors found the "toolkit" metaphor to be an appropriate title for activity two. However there are many other metaphors that could be used in its place (e.g. leadership backpack, file cabinet). Ultimately, instructors should utilize the metaphor they find most apt and relatable to students.

Meredith A. Smith is an area coordinator at Fairfield University where she practices leadership development with the resident assistants, orientation leaders, and students living in her residential communities. Meredith holds a BA from Wellesley College and a MA from the University of Maryland, where she served as a member of the Multi-Institutional Study of Leadership research team, resulting in presentations of research studies at national student affairs conferences and a coauthored article on mentorship and leadership.

Tyler L. McClain is assistant director of student programs and leadership development at Fairfield University, where he is responsible for facilitation and development of leadership programs for the Division of Student Affairs, working closely with many faculty and staff offices. Tyler holds a BA from Johnson and Wales University and a MS from the University of Rhode Island in human development and family studies with a concentration in college student personnel.

Active Learning Module 9a

Understanding Complex Organizations

Dave Dessauer

> Summary of Concepts

This module addresses Chapter 9, Understanding and Renewing Complex Organizations. In this section, students explore the nature of organizations as complex systems affected by structural, historical, and cultural influences. Organizations are complex systems that comprise a collection of groups that exist to achieve a specific purpose. The role of leadership in an organization is to help the groups within it engage with one another in an effective manner.

> Learning Outcomes

Students will

- Understand organizations as complex systems
- Be able to analyze a complex organization
- Consider the role of leadership within a complex organization

› Module Overview

Lead students through an activity requiring collaborative effort followed by discussion about how the systemic nature of an organization creates complexity. Students then analyze a complex organization. By conducting online research of an organization, students assess the elements that orient it, including mission, vision, and core values. Students analyze how an organization's guiding statements, structure, and culture reflect achieving a stated purpose. Students then connect this to their own experiences within organizations.

Estimated Time
Activity 1: Lower the Bar, 10-minute activity, 10-minute reflective discussion
Activity 2: Organizational Analysis, 20-minute activity, 20-minute presentation and discussion

Materials/Supplies
Yardstick (or equivalent such as a broom stick, PVC pipe, or foam noodle)
Computer, laptop, or tablet

› Module Activities

Activity 1: Lower the Bar

Time: 20 minutes

Explain to students that the purpose of this activity is to explore the how the systemic nature of organizations can impact the outcome of a collective effort.

- Divide students into groups of eight.
- Each group should form two even lines with members facing each other.

- Explain the objective is to work together to raise a stick as high as possible before lowering it to the ground while maintaining contact with the stick the entire time.
- Instruct students to extend their index fingers at waist level.
- Lay the stick across the tops of students' fingers and instruct the groups to begin.
- The group must start over if contact with the stick is broken.

Processing questions:

- Was your group able to accomplish the objective of lowering the bar to the ground?
- What aspects of this activity were easy? What aspects of this activity were challenging?
- Does this activity relate to ways the manner in which organizations function?
- Can you think of an example of an action or decision that had unintended effect within an organization?

This exemplifies working within a system. Organizations by nature are a system. When all parts are connected, one movement impacts the rest. Even simple tasks, like lowering a stick can, become more challenging. This demonstrates the complex nature of organizations. Ask students to provide examples of a complex organization.

Facilitator Notes   The simple nature of this activity can be deceiving. Students will find little challenge in raising the stick. Lowering the stick to the ground presents a more difficult task. The upward pressure from the fingers attempting to keep in contact with the stick causes it to rise, foiling the group's efforts. Groups may initially be humored but may grow frustrated as the activity progresses. Even the smallest unexpected action can cause the stick to inadvertently rise. Begin processing after groups have had several attempts to complete the activity.

Activity 2: Organizational Analysis

Time: 30 minutes

Continuing with the existing small groups, have each select a complex organization to analyze. Define a complex organization as an entity of more than 20 people that comprises groups of groups that exist to achieve a specific purpose. The small groups should conduct an Internet search of websites, wiki's, or blogs related to the organization; analyze available information on the organization's purpose, structure, culture, and operation; and present their findings to all the groups. Provide the follow the following questions to guide students' exploration:

- *Mission*: Why does this organization exist?
- *Vision*: What is the ideal future for this organization?
- *Core values*: What actions or beliefs guide action and behavior in this organization?
- *Size*: How large is the organization? How many people are part of, or work for, this organization? How is the organization structured?
- *Culture*: What can be inferred about the organization's culture from the information collected?
- *Operation*: Why can this organization be considered complex? How does this organization operate? Where does it operate? How does it work to achieve its stated purpose? Are there any factors that increase the complexity of this organization's operation?

Allow each group to present their analysis. Encourage groups to share any discoveries about the organization. Following the presentation, lead a reflective discussion.

- Which organization was the most interesting? Why?
- Of what organization would you want to be a member or employee? Why?

- How are the structure, function, and culture of an organization impacted by it mission?
- What role does leadership play in a complex organization?
- Concluding this discussion, what is the most essential component of an organization?

Facilitator Notes   Consider assigning an organization for each group to analyze. This ensures that a variety of organizations with unique purposes, structures, and cultures will be discussed. Examples of organizations to assign include Kiva, Southwest Airlines, Tom's Shoes, Google, Boeing, the Khan Academy, Gallup, Zappos, Amazon.com, IBM, Lockheed Martin, and Timberland. Another option would be to explore local organizations, such as your college or university or the local government (including all commissions, councils, and neighborhood associations).

Dave Dessauer is the coordinator for cocurricular leadership programs in the Adele H. Stamp Student Union–Center for Campus Life at the University of Maryland. Dave received his MA in higher education administration from Louisiana State University.

Organizational Culture

Kerry Priest

> Summary of Concepts

This module addresses Chapter 9, Understanding and Renewing Complex Organizations. In this section, students explore organizational culture, organizational networks, life cycles of organizations, multicultural organizational development, and learning in organizations. The central theme is that complex organizations have influence—they influence the life and learning of members within the organization and influence people and groups outside of the organization through network interactions. The more that leaders understand the culture, connections, and cycles of organizations, the greater their ability to encourage all members to take an active role in accomplishing organizational goals. The best organizations are those in which members are continually learning and growing in order to stay relevant and adaptive to new challenges.

> Learning Outcomes

Students will

- Identify and describe aspects of organizational culture
- Understand the role leaders play in creating organizational culture
- Apply concepts of organizational learning to their own organizations

> Module Overview

Students use a "campus tour" scenario to identify and describe organizational culture. The subsequent discussion allows student to connect their observations with cultural frameworks and reflect on the role of leaders in creating culture.

Students then discuss how creating culture and cultural change is achieved through organizational learning, and they generate strategies for enhancing learning within the organizations they lead.

Estimated Time
Activity 1: Campus Culture Survey
- Scenario discussion and poster creation: 20 minutes
- Group presentations: 15 minutes
- Reflective discussion: 10 minutes
Activity 2: Connection to Learning Organizations
- Pair/small group discussion: 10 minutes
- Large group debrief: 5 minutes

Materials/Supplies
Flip charts: one per group for summarizing and presenting observations
Markers

Printed copies of scenario and observation questions, one per person

Board or flip chart to write down major points that emerge from discussion

› Module Activities

Activity 1: Campus Culture Survey

Time: 40–45 minutes

Divide students into groups of four to six. Give each student a copy of the following scenario:

Your friend is a high school senior who is considering coming to [Your University] next year. When they come to campus for a visit, you volunteer to accompany them on the campus tour and orientation activities of the day. During the tour, you begin to notice some cues and clues of the campus culture. Make observations about the campus culture by answering the following questions:

- What do you physically "see" while on a campus visit?
- What are the structures and processes of the campus that are visible?
- What values seem to be important to your school?
- What do students hear about or see during their visit that communicates ideals, goals, values, and aspirations of the school?
- Who are considered role models around here? Whose actions are recognized and rewarded for high standards of performance?
- What are the formal or informal guidelines for "how life works" around here? Are there certain ways people dress, talk, or act?
- What might be some of the underlying assumptions that drive the values and actions of the school (of faculty, staff, or current students?)

Ask students to discuss the scenario and questions within their groups, and announce that they have 15–20 minutes to create a poster (frame it as creating a "campus recruitment brochure") that outlines or illustrates the key aspects of campus culture. Depending on the total number of groups, instruct students that each group will give a one- to three-minute overview of their key points back to the rest of the class. After each group has shared their presentations, facilitate a whole group discussion, utilizing the debriefing questions.

Debriefing Questions

- What were the strongest aspects of culture represented through these presentations? Why do you think some aspects stood out more than others?
- How do your observations represent or connect to the cultural frameworks presented in the book?
  - Schein's three levels: artifacts, espoused beliefs, assumptions
  - Deal and Kennedy's framework: values, heroes, rites and rituals, communication networks
  - Bolman and Deal's four frames: structural, human resource, political, symbolic
  - Hofstede's cultural dimensions: power distance, individualism, masculinity, uncertainty avoidance, long-range orientation
- How do you think campus culture influences students' decisions to become (or not to become) part of the organization or campus? Are all aspects of the culture positive for everyone?
- Do the cultural aspects identified represent a multicultural organization? Why or why not?
- What is your role as a leader in creating culture (on the campus as a whole or within the clubs and groups of which you are a part)?

Variations   The scenario can be adapted to fit a variety of situations, such as interviewing for graduate school, taking on an advising role for an organization, or visiting an organization as a potential employee. This is also a great opportunity for a group field trip. If time allows, you could actually ask students to sign up for a campus tour or observe a new student orientation and take observational field notes. Even sending the individuals "outside" for 10–15 minutes to take notes on what they see around the building or in local area could help generate a list of cultural cues and clues.

Many colleges and universities have recruitment videos posted on their school website. Showing a recruitment clip may help set context for identifying aspects of culture. Analyzing school websites, as well as printed brochures and other documents used by the organization could be another form of cultural analysis. (E.g., How do these forms of communication illustrate aspects of organizational culture?)

Activity 2: Connection to Learning Organizations

Time: 15–20 minutes

Discuss the connection between creating culture and learning organizations:

- The culture of an organization impacts our ability to create change; and as we seek to change cultures we influence both individuals within our organization and those whom our organization serves or influences.
- To be a change agent requires continual learning; continuous learning by both leaders and participants in organizations is of critical importance.

Ask students to review Exhibit 9.4: Ways Leaders Can Enhance Organizational Learning in the text. Ask students to identify the organization in which they are most involved and capture this list on a white board or flip chart. In pairs or small groups, have students discuss the following (approximately five minutes):

- How committed is your organization to learning?
- Why is learning valuable for the context, situation, or goals of your group?
- What challenges does your organization face?
- What are some strategies to improve learning?

Gather students back together in a large-group debrief, asking students to highlight common challenges, share best-practices, and offer ideas for improvement.

> Facilitator Notes

The campus survey activity assumes that students have experienced a campus tour or orientation session or that they have enough campus experience from which to make observations about the culture. The activity challenges them to view campus through the lens of an "outsider," all the while having "insider" status. If this challenges students, you may need to provide some initial examples of culture (e.g., *types of clothing, common terms or slang, important buildings*). While the first activity challenges students to consider the larger organization they belong to (campus), the second activity asks them to really focus on a smaller group in which they are invested as a leader or member. If a student does not feel connected to a campus organization, encourage them to consider their workplace, residence hall, recreational sports team, or other related organization.

Kerry Priest is an assistant professor in the School of Leadership Studies at Kansas State University. Kerry received her PhD from Virginia Tech, with a research focus on learning communities and leadership identity development.

Active Learning Module 10a

Understanding Individual Change

Jillian Volpe White

> ## Summary of Concepts

This module addresses Chapter 10, Understanding Change. In this section, students explore change from an individual perspective, particularly about different types of change and how the scope of a change can invoke a variety of individual responses. A change can be a small adjustment or a deep, transformational experience that reframes organizational values and practices. Individual responses to change vary and the model of individual reactions to change depends upon whether this change was perceived to be positive or negative. Change may occur slowly over time or suddenly, as when something reaches a "tipping point" and becomes widespread very quickly. In order to facilitate change in an organization, students must understand how individuals experience change and how they manage themselves during a transition.

> Learning Outcomes

Students will

- Understand the stages individuals experience during a change process
- Consider their own response to change and how they can be well suited for change experiences

> Module Overview

Students will explore the campus using identifying features from the past and the present. Lead the group in a discussion about the hazards of navigating a place with an old map and changing conceptions of situations or themselves through the change process.

Students will reflect on a personal change, how they were supported during that transition, and the stages they went through in adopting that change as part of their self-concept. Students will develop a visual representation of their change and discuss strategies for managing future changes.

Estimated Time

Activity 1: Navigating Campus
- Group activity: 5 minutes
- Debriefing discussion: 10 minutes

Activity 2: Personal Change Inventory
- Individual reflection: 10 minutes
- Creative reflection: 10 minutes
- Small group sharing: 10 minutes
- Directed discussion: 10 minutes

Materials/Supplies
Paper
Pens or pencils

Current and historical pictures of a few campus buildings
Labels with the names of campus departments or functions
Markers
Magazines
Glue
Scissors

> Module Activities

Activity 1: Navigating Campus

Time: 15 minutes

Choose five to eight well-known campus buildings and print a picture of each building. On strips of paper, write the current function of each building. On another strip of paper, write the past function of each building. For example, the Smith building might currently be a theater but in the past was a gym. Display the pictures or names of campus buildings around the room. If your campus is newer or the functions of buildings have not changed, choose buildings that would be familiar in your city or region.

Explain to students that this activity is about examining how we understand change from an individual perspective. Pass out the strips of paper with the current function of each building and ask students to match the function to the building. Then pass out the strips of paper with the past function of each building and ask students to match these to the same buildings.

Debriefing Questions
- What did you observe during this activity?
- What would happen if someone tried to navigate campus today with a map from the past?
- Can you think of a time when you tried to use an old belief or idea to understand a new situation? What happened?
- What steps are required to change our understanding of a situation or ourselves as part of the change process?

Activity Variation   Instead of having students match functions to buildings on campus or in your city, show them a current map of a city and a past map of a city. Ask them to compare the maps and point out the differences between them.

Activity 2: Personal Change Inventory

Time: 40 minutes

In order to facilitate organizational change, students need to understand change from the individual perspective. Schlossberg identifies four potential resources for managing change: the situation, yourself, supports, and strategies for coping. One way for students to understand how they manage change is take an inventory of how they have responded to a past change.

Have students think of a significant personal change that occurred in their life. Give students about 10 minutes to respond to the following questions regarding the change they identified:

- What happened?
- How did you feel?
- What past experiences were you able to draw on to help you navigate this change?
- What people or resources were useful?
- What coping strategies did you utilize?
- What phases did you go through in order for this change to become a part of your life?

After students have answered the questions about their personal change, they will use these responses to develop a representation of their change. Using their answers to the questions, students will create a visual representation that reflects their personal change and transition. Students can create a drawing, diagram, collage, or other object. Give students about 10 minutes to create their visual representation.

In pairs or small groups, have students share their visual representation. After students have had a chance to share in pairs or small groups, invite them back to the large group for discussion.

Debriefing Questions

- What did you observe about how you manage change?
- What similar phases did you experience as part of your change?
- What sources of support did you identify that aided you in making the change?
- Looking ahead, how might these resources be useful in making future changes?

Activity Variation   Instead of having the students share their visual representations in pairs or small groups, create a gallery of their work by displaying it on the walls. Allow students time to peruse the gallery before engaging in a large group discussion about what they observed in the artwork.

> Facilitator Notes

Be prepared for some students who feel comfortable doing so to share very personal change experiences.

Jillian Volpe White is a community engagement coordinator at the Florida State University Center for Leadership and Social Change. She also teaches in the undergraduate certificate in leadership studies.

Active Learning Module 10b

Facilitating Change in Organizations

Sarah Edwards

❯ Summary of Concepts

This module addresses Chapter 10, Understanding Change. In this section, students explore the complex nature of influencing organizational change. For any lasting change to occur, leaders must help group members move beyond what is comfortable and embrace the risk of the unknown. Just as individuals do, organizations must feel a compelling sense of need in order to embrace the sometimes painful change process.

❯ Learning Outcomes

Students will

- Understand the complex nature of leading organizational change
- Consider what risks the organization is and is not willing to take in pursuit of change
- Apply Kotter's Eight-Stage Process of Creating Major Change to organizational change goals

> Module Overview

Students first explore well-known statements about change in terms of their connections to Chapter Ten of *Exploring Leadership* (3rd edition). Then they develop action plans for change in a group they are a part of using Kotter's Eight-Stage Process.

Estimated Time

Activity 1: Understanding Change, 25–30 minutes
- Large group discussion: 5 minutes
- Small group discussion of quotes: 5–10 minutes
- Reporting out and large group facilitation: 15 minutes

Activity 2: Creating Change, 25–35 minutes
- Large group discussion: 5–10 minutes
- Small group discussion: 15 minutes
- Reporting out and large group facilitation: 5–10 minutes

Materials/Supplies

Printed or written handouts of each of the eight quotes
Board or flip charts and markers to write down major points
    emerging from the discussion
Handouts of Kotter's Eight-Stage Process
Notecards for students to write on

> Module Activities

Activity 1: Understanding Change

Time: 25–30 minutes
    Facilitate the large group in answering the following questions:

- Why is change important in the leadership process?
- What are the challenges of facilitating change?

Divide students into eight groups and give each one of the following quotations. Have students spend 5–10 minutes exploring what the quote means in relation to the chapter.

- "The world as we have created it is a process of our thinking. It cannot be changed without changing our thinking."—Albert Einstein
- "If you want change, you have to make it. If we want progress we have to drive it."—Susan Rice
- "They always say time changes things, but you actually have to change them yourself."—Andy Warhol
- "Sometimes good things fall apart so better things can fall together."—Marilyn Monroe
- "He who rejects change is the architect of decay. The only human institution which rejects progress is the cemetery."—Harold Wilson
- "It's not that some people have willpower and some don't. It's that some people are ready to change and others are not."—James Gordon
- "There is nothing like returning to a place that remains unchanged to find the ways in which you yourself have altered."—Nelson Mandela
- "Change your thoughts and you change your world."—Norman Vincent Peale
- "Man cannot discover new oceans unless he has the courage to lose sight of the shore."—Andre Gide
- "In a chronically leaking boat, energy devoted to changing vessels is more productive than energy devoted to patching leaks."—Warren Buffett

Ask each group to discuss their statement and then share with the larger group. Facilitation points for each statement to explore include

- "The world as we have created it is a process of our thinking. It cannot be changed without changing our thinking."—Albert Einstein
  - In order to facilitate effective change, we have to change the way we think about the organization.
  - It is important to think outside of the box and let go of assumptions about the organization and its members in order to see what could be.
- "If you want change, you have to make it. If we want progress we have to drive it."—Susan Rice
  - Change agents have to be willing to take risks if they want others to be willing to do so.
- "They always say time changes things, but you actually have to change them yourself."—Andy Warhol
  - For successful change to occur, people need to create a sense of urgency, not just wait for change to happen.
- "Sometimes good things fall apart so better things can fall together."—Marilyn Monroe
  - Change involves a willingness to let go of things that aren't failing as well as things that are in the hopes of achieving greater outcomes.
  - Some people approach change with an idea that only the "failing" areas are going to be altered, but deep change impacts the whole organization.
- "He who rejects change is the architect of decay. The only human institution which rejects progress is the cemetery."—Harold Wilson
  - Change-resistant organizations aren't actually staying the same, they're slowly deteriorating.
- "It's not that some people have willpower and some don't. It's that some people are ready to change and others are not."—James Gordon

- Change is scary, and people resist it for many reasons, including satisfaction, fear, self-interest, lack of self-confidence, myopia, and habit.
- "Man cannot discover new oceans unless he has the courage to lose sight of the shore."—Andre Gide
  - The risk of change relies on being able to find opportunities and avoid hazards while heading into new territory.
- "In a chronically leaking boat, energy devoted to changing vessels is more productive than energy devoted to patching leaks."—Warren Buffett
  - Sometimes organizations spend far more time and energy on not changing due to fear or lack of vision than it would take to step back and see what could be altered to find a new, successful plan.

Activity 2: Creating Change

Time: 25–35 minutes

In one large group, facilitate a discussion to identify an organization of interest to everyone. This might be a student organization or campus department they are all familiar with or the college/university as an institution.

Then discuss the following questions and note responses on a whiteboard or flip chart.

- What are some change goals we would have for this organization?
- What are some obstacles this organization faces?
- What are some of the assets and strengths the organization has to build upon?
- What are the risks associated with this change?

Divide the students into small groups to address the goals listed in the last discussion. Depending on the number of change goals identified, you can give one to each group, or have some groups share the same change goal. In their small groups, direct students to create an action plan following Kotter's Eight-Stage Process from Chapter Ten of *Exploring Leadership* (3rd edition).

Circulate around the small groups to challenge students to go deeper on each step of the model. After each group has developed their plan, have them report back to the large group. After each team has presented their action plan, reflect as a large group on the similarities and differences in each action plan and discuss the overarching implications of navigating obstacles and risks for the whole group.

Activity Variation   This activity could also apply to a real or fictitious case study of an organization needing to implement change. In that case, either provide the students with the goals, obstacles, and risks ahead of time or allow for extra time for the students to become familiar with the scenario to then be able to create those elements.

Sarah Edwards is a senior advisor with the Student Government Association in the Department of Student Activities at Texas A&M University. Sarah is working on her PhD in higher education—organizational leadership at Azusa Pacific University with a research focus on leadership development, strengths, and gender identity.

Active Learning Module 11a

Social Change Model of Leadership Development

Antron Mahoney

> ## Summary of Concepts

This module addresses Chapter 11, Strategies for Change. In this section, students explore the Social Change Model of Leadership Development, also known as the "7 Cs" model. Students learn about the values that are essential for creating positive social change as they work at the individual, group, and society or community levels. Furthermore, the Social Change Model emphasizes the reciprocal, interconnected dynamic of these three perspective levels.

The model incorporates the following key assumptions:

- Leadership involves effecting change for the greater good.
- Leadership is a collaborative and relational process.
- Leadership is value-focused.
- All students are potential leaders; not just those who hold formal positions.
- Service is an effective learning experience for developing students' leadership skills.

> Learning Outcomes

Students will

- Be able to describe the Social Change Model
- Understand the reciprocal interaction between the three value-based perspective levels described in the Social Change Model
- Be able to articulate how the model relates to their personal leadership experiences

> Module Overview

Students work together in groups to create a collaborative song. By debriefing that team experience, students discuss the values of the social change model and alignment with their collaborative leadership experiences.

Estimated Time

Activity 1: Students Create Individual Sounds, 15 minutes

Activity 2: Students Create and Perform Group Songs, 25 minutes

Activity 3: Debriefing the Experience, 10 minutes

Activity 4: Connection to Theory and Practice, 10 minutes

Materials/Supplies

Board or flip charts with markers to write down major points emerging from discussion

Diagram of the Social Change Model of Leadership Development on board or flip chart

Handout with list of the 7 Cs defined

> Module Activities

Activity 1: Individual Sounds

Time: 15 minutes

Explain to students that you will be exploring the Social Change Model of Leadership Development from the Chapter 11 reading. As students engage in the exercise, they should try to be aware of correlations in the activity related to leadership in this context.

Ask the students to form a circle. As a way to begin and introduce themselves, students should share their name and a sound that represents them in some way. It could be any type of noise, sound, or rhythm.

Encourage students to use the first sound that comes to mind. As a way to role model, share your name and sound first. Once you have shared, go around the circle until each student has shared her or his sound.

For some students, identifying a sound will be easy, and for others, the task may be challenging. Likewise, some students may receive unsolicited help from other students. Observe these dynamics. It will be helpful for later discussion.

Activity 2: Group Songs

Time: 25 minutes

Students will now form small groups and create a song using only the sounds that each member of their small group presented in the circle. The song can be an original or a rendition of a popular song. Observe the students' reaction to your announcement. It will be helpful for later discussion.

Have students form small groups by counting off. Limit group size to no more than six students. You will not participate in this phase of the activity.

Students will have approximately five minutes to create their song before performing it for the entire group. Suggest that groups spread out from one another, or if possible, gather in different locations.

After the appropriate time, call the groups back together. Have each group perform their song as the others watch and support.

Activity 3: Debriefing the Experience

Time: 10 minutes

Debrief each phase of the exercise with the group:

- What was it like identifying a sound and sharing it? Easy or difficult? Why?
- What was the process like within your small group creating the song? What was your initial reaction when the assignment was given? What made this process challenging? How did you work through the challenges?
- What consideration did your group give to the audience while preparing for the performance? What was it like to perform the song in front of everyone?

While debriefing, note any of your personal observations from the exercise the students do not mention that could be relevant to the Social Change Model.

Activity 4: Connection to Theory and Practice

Time: 10 minutes

Discuss connections to the *Exploring Leadership* reading:

- How did the exercise reflect what you read about the Social Change Model of Leadership Development?
- How were the 7 Cs represented in this exercise?

- How were the feedback loops represented in the exercise?
- How did this exercise and the Social Change Model relate to your past leadership experiences?

Refer to the Social Change Model diagram as needed. Pass out the handout with the 7 Cs defined.

> Facilitator Notes

Be prepared to assist students in connecting how elements of the activity could be related to the Social Change Model and leadership experiences. For example, the activity of presenting a sound denotes the individual perspective level of the Social Change Model. When some students have a hard time coming up with a sound, this could reflect the challenge and process of understanding individual strengths and values.

Furthermore, using the eclectic group of sounds to create a song will seem impossible to some students at first. However, once students create the songs they recognize that the diversity of sounds is what makes it possible to develop a unique song. This can be correlated to the ideas of diversity, inclusivity, collaboration, and common purpose. Moreover, developing and performing songs that take the audience into consideration signifies creating change that addresses a community need.

Antron Mahoney is assistant director of the Center for Leadership and Social Change at Florida State University, where he is responsible for developing and implementing leadership development programs. He also teaches in the Undergraduate Certificate in Leadership Studies Program.

Active Learning Module 11b

Building Coalitions for Collective Action

Wendy Wagner

> Summary of Concepts

This module addresses Chapter 11, Strategies for Change. In this section, students learn about building coalitions of organizations to accomplish large-scale change. Change agents are leaders committed to social justice beyond their own organization to building trans-organizational coalitions for collective action. While we often think of politicians, civil servants, researchers, and opinion leaders as leading change efforts at the community or societal level, students and others at the grass roots have an opportunity to influence large-scale social change through coalitions.

Coalitions strengthen strategic planning and enable groups to achieve successes that no one organization or group can accomplish alone. The establishment of coalitions involves creating a strong core group, establishing accountability by constantly checking assumptions, and acknowledging personal and organizational goals for making change. The content presented here is focused on campus-community collaborations and has a social justice framework; it can be adapted for on-campus coalition building around other approaches to service.

> Learning Outcomes

Students will

- Identify coalition building practices
- Be able to describe concrete steps to develop a coalition
- Apply the concepts related to coalition building to address a specific social issue

> Module Overview

Students select a social change issue and discuss the issues related to coalition building in relation to that specific case. Working in small groups, they then use a worksheet to guide them through the steps of creating a coalition.

Estimated Time
Activity 1: Select a Social Issue and Potential Ways to Address It, 15 minutes
Activity 2: Benefits and Drawbacks of Coalition Building, 45 minutes

Materials/Supplies
Flip chart paper and markers or a whiteboard and markers

> Module Activities

Activity 1: Select a Social Issue and Potential Ways to Address It

Time: 15 minutes

As a large group, have students list the social issues they are interested in confronting. From this list, have them select one overarching issue they are interested in exploring for the duration of the session.

Ask students to describe the ways they are or could be confronting the issue. Help them think broadly about efforts for change, including community service, advocacy, lobbying for policy change, educating others about the issue, boycotting, and so on. As you go, have them distinguish among types of efforts:

- Individual efforts and group efforts
- Efforts to address the needs created by the problem and efforts to create change (for example, supporting a food bank or building a homeless shelter versus lobbying for higher wages for low-income workers so people can afford their own food and shelter)
- Focus of change at the local level (in a specific community) and focus of change at the national or global level

Remind students that for any given social issue, there are a variety of organizations working to address it in their own way. Thinking about the social issue they just selected as a group, have students generate a list of the types of organizations that might address it in a variety of ways. You may need to help students consider a wider range of organizations beyond nonprofit service and advocacy organizations that exist specifically to address the issue. For example, are there faith-based organizations or houses of worship that may address the issue? Are there service-learning courses at this college or university that address this topic? Is there conceivably a local government commission or task force addressing the issue? Is it possible there is a state-level congressman who believes in addressing this issue by providing grant funding? Try to have at least one example of a for-profit organization on the list (for example, a for-profit apartment complex that includes several affordably priced units for low-wage working families, or a corporate foundation that might be a source of funding).

Describe coalition building as how these organizations come to take unified, coordinated action.

Activity 2: Benefits and Drawbacks of Coalition Building

Time: 45 minutes

Divide students into small groups, assigning one of the organizations listed in the last activity to each one.

As a warm-up discussion, the small groups will first talk about what a variety of coalitions among all the organizations represented here might look like. Refer to Mizrahi and Rosenthal's (1993) four types of coalitions based on specific or general goal and duration of the coalition. Draw a two-by-two grid on the board (or flip chart paper) and have students suggest examples for each quadrant related to the social change goal they chose earlier. Students may need help in some quadrants. For examples, refer students to Exhibit 11.5: Campus Coalitions, in *Exploring Leadership* (3rd edition).

Example

	Short-Term Time Frame	Long-Term Time Frame
Specific goals	Example: Respond to the need for emergency hypothermia shelter for the homeless population in a particular community this winter.	Example: Respond to a particular community's ongoing need to shelter people without homes during periods of extreme heat or cold.
General goals	Example: Respond to the broad range of needs of individuals and families without homes this holiday season.	Example: Work to end homelessness in this community.

Have each small group describe their grids to the larger group. Next have each small group discuss the potential benefits of a coalition with the organizations represented in the room: What would we gain by working with some of the other groups here? As the students work on these lists, circulate around the room, helping students think about new angles. Some general benefits are listed here (encourage students to think specifically about this issue and the organizations represented by other small groups):

- Gain skills, knowledge, and expertise
- Gain access to funding
- Gain access to people in positions of power, like people in local or state government who can navigate how to make change related to policies or laws
- Capitalize on the connections that others have (access to more volunteers or potential donors)
- Capitalize on the resources others have (access to buildings, equipment, existing processes like petition drives)

Give the groups 10 minutes to generate their lists, and have them share with the larger group.

Then have each small group discuss the potential drawbacks of a coalition with the organizations represented in the room: What are the risks of a coalition with some of the other groups here? Again, circulate to help students think from the perspective of the organization they represent and some of the likely individuals in that organization. Refer students to some of the issues raised in Chapter Eleven.

- *The tension of autonomy and accountability*: Right now, our organization can make its own choices. Agreeing to work with others means we may need to put the coalition's priorities over our own at times.
- *The tension of mixed loyalties*: What if our members prioritize the goals of the coalition over the goals of our organization?

- *The tension of relationships and results*: How do we know whether the other organizations are interested in a short-term win or in a long-term relationship which will have some wins and losses over time?
- *The tension of unity and diversity*: Will our voice be heard? Groups that would represent smaller numbers or less political power might be exploited or co-opted.
- *The issue of trust*: There is a chance that some groups might have other motives and are only claiming commitment to this issue. (Students may need help here. Politicians may want to be able to claim this commitment during an election year but won't really offer us any actual help. Corporations may offer lip service in order to get access to our people resources or the good will they receive by claiming to work with us.)

Invite small groups to share with the larger group. Conclude with the students' own thoughts about weighing the potential benefits and drawbacks.

Finally, have students create a list of the particular leadership skills involved in coalition building. Some examples might include the ability to think broadly about being inclusive about potential partners, being able to build relationships across those diverse groups, or being persuasive in order to bring those organizations to a larger movement.

❯ Reference

Mizrahi, T., & Rosenthal, B. S. (1993). Managing dynamic tensions in social change coalitions. In T. Mizrahi & J. Morrison (Eds.), *Community organization and social administration: Advances, trends and emerging principles* (pp. 11–40). New York, NY: Haworth Press.

Wendy Wagner is an assistant professor of leadership and community engagement at George Mason University. She is also the director of Mason's Center for Leadership and Community Engagement.

Active Learning Module 11c

From Service to Civic Engagement

Jennifer M. Pigza

> Summary of Concepts

This module addresses Chapter 11, Strategies for Change. In this section, students explore several theoretical frameworks and practical ideas for creating the change that they seek. This chapter presents several change-making strategies, including

- Engaging with allies and advocates
- Change-making through community service
- Navigating conflict
- Identifying passions
- Recognizing opportunities for change (timing and locales)

The chapter also places the Relational Leadership Model in conversation with the Social Change Model to elucidate differences. "Leadership, according to the Relational Leadership Model, involved the components of process and purpose by being ethical, empowering, and inclusive. The Social Change Model proposes a dynamic interplay between the sets of personal, group, and societal values."

Frequently students who are engaged in community service as a change-making strategy are drawn to advocate systemic change related to their issue of concern. This module is designed to help students extend their efforts for change from service to civic engagement. It helps students move from passion about direct action to the development of communication strategies for social justice advocacy and civic engagement (developed by Nash, 2010). These communication strategies are applicable across the change-making environments and processes mentioned in Chapter 11.

› Learning Outcomes

Students will

- Consider how their own direct service efforts can lead to social justice advocacy and civic engagement
- Learn about communication strategies for social justice advocacy
- Reflect upon their own preferred communication strategies for change

› Module Overview

This module has three movements. Students engage in a group discussion about the relationships among community service, civic engagement, social justice, and change-making. Then through two simulated fishbowl-style conversations, students speak about a current issue by role-playing different communication strategies. Finally students engage in a closing conversation in which they weave advocacy strategies into their emerging sense of leadership.

Estimated Time

Activity 1: Opening Conversation, 10 minutes

Activity 2: Fishbowl-Style Advocacy Simulation

- First simulation, 10 minutes
- Reveal of advocacy types, 10 minutes
- Second simulation, 10 minutes
- Debrief, 10 minutes

Activity 3: Closing Conversation, 10 minutes

Materials/Supplies

Slips of paper with the titles and brief descriptions of each type of advocacy (one slip/role per student)

Brief description of the issue to be discussed

Handout with summary of five types of advocacy (provided) *or* copies of Nash article

> Module Activities

Before students arrive to the session, arrange the chairs into two concentric circles—an inner circle with five to seven chairs and the remaining chairs on the perimeter.

Activity 1: Opening Conversation

Time: 10 minutes

This opening conversation invites students to discuss the connections among community service, civic engagement, social justice, and change-making. Begin by writing these four ideas on the board, and ask very open-ended questions, such as: How do these relate in your experience? How did Chapter 11 help us understand the relationships among them? Follow up with questions that lead students to the topic of communication strategies for social justice/civic engagement, such as: What happens when you have tried to move your service to civic engagement? When you have tried to translate your passion for an issue to advocating policy change? What kind of communication works best for you?...Today's module will expose you to different communication strategies for civic engagement.

Activity 2: Fishbowl-Style Advocacy Simulation

Time: 40 minutes

First Simulation, 10 minutes   Explain to students that the group will engage in a simulated discussion about a current topic that you have chosen in advance. Possible topics include upcoming ballot measures, campus-based policy issues, current events. Each student receives a description of the issue, for example a ballot initiative summary, brief newspaper/web article, or editorial. Choose an issue that students can easily grasp and for which they are likely to have an opinion. If you suspect that there may not be sufficient pro and con opinions about the issue or to allow for anonymity of personal opinion, assign positions as well as types of advocacy. For example, identify both a pro-radvocate and a con-radvocate.

In the center circle of chairs, place the brief descriptions of the types of advocacy face down. Ask for volunteers to take these chairs and then randomly assign the remaining students the types of advocacy by distributing the slips of paper. Ask the students in the center circle to talk about the issue in their assigned roles. Encourage a spirited, over-the-top interpretation of their roles. Remind all students to keep their role identities private.

Reveal of Advocacy types, 10 minutes   After several minutes of conversation, stop the simulation. Ask students if they can characterize the types of arguments they heard in the simulation. Appeals to logic? Personal story? Emotional pleas? Conciliation? Current event junkie? Polemic attack? Anger? Ask students to turn to Activity 2: Social Justice Advocacy in the Workbook, which describes the five communication strategies. Review them briefly. Ask the students to guess which roles were present in the center circle.

Second Simulation, 10 minutes   Now that everyone knows the strategies of advocacy, ask a new group of students to take the center circle to continue the conversation. The purpose of the second simulation is to allow different students to voice the types and for the types to be more fully expressed. Stop the conversation with enough time to debrief and do the closing activity.

Debrief, 10 minutes   In debriefing the simulation, return to the main connections between this activity and Chapter Eleven—strategies for change involve strategies for communication, and moving from service to civic engagement requires that we become skilled in advocacy. Generally debrief the experience with questions such as: How did it feel to play a certain type of advocacy? Do you see these strategies for communication in your environment? Where and how? Is one strategy more natural for you than others? What situations and environments call for which types of advocacy? Can you think of anyone who exemplifies being a gladvocate? Be sure to remind students that although the gladvocate is the most balanced of strategies, they all have their uses depending on the environment and purpose.

Activity 3: Closing Conversation

Time: 10 minutes

In closing, invite students to talk about their own experiences of being an advocate for change and of being in conversations around contestable topics such as described today. How does their growing sense of leadership connect to the way they strive to make change? What is one take-away they have from today's experience?

> Facilitator Notes

The Nash (2010) article is likely available in full-text through your institution's library. These ideas also received full book-length treatment (Nash, Johnson & Murray, 2012).

In choosing a topic for the simulation, strive to identify a topic that will have enough contested terrain and nuance for a good conversation. Campus-based, local, and global issues could all work; choose a topic that does not require too much prior knowledge. Students may have a difficult time getting into their roles in the beginning of the simulation. You may need to assure them and the group that they are acting according to role, not necessarily personal opinion.

For a variation on the simulation, engage in one longer simulation rather than two. If offering only one simulation, have the center circle start the conversation and after 5–10 minutes invite other students to "tag" into the conversation. This allows students a longer conversation, which may get deeper into the issues, and allows students individual choice about when to join it.

> References

Nash, R. J. (2010, May-June). What is the best way to be a social justice advocate? Communication strategies for effective social justice advocacy. *About Campus, 15,* 11–18.

Nash, R. J., Johnson, R. G., & Murray, M. C. (2012). *Teaching college students communication strategies for effective social justice advocacy.* New York: Peter Lang.

Jennifer M. Pigza is the chair of the graduate program in Leadership for Social Justice and the associate director of the Catholic Institute for Lasallian Social Action (CILSA) at Saint Mary's College of California. She has invested nearly 20 years in advancing social justice education and community service-learning in higher education.

Five Communication Styles for Social Justice Advocacy

Radvocate	Madvocate
Ideas are in the extreme ends of the ideological continuum Helps get to the roots of issues Offers solid analysis "Voice crying out in the desert" Can appear self-righteous	Operates from anger, indignation, moral outrage Shocks people out of lethargy and into awareness and action Can silence those who think differently May create enemies, not allies

Sadvocate	Fadvocate
Convinces through sad, subjective self-disclosures Can invite empathy and compassion Rather than rally to action, this may evoke a sense of pity and victimization	Excited about the cause du jour Keeps others educated about current issues Scant commitment to long-term engagement

Gladvocate	Personal Qualities Associated with Gladvocacy
Teaches through invitation, generosity Calls people together to listen and grow in understanding Tenuous tenacity—committed, yet open to dialogue Helps discover overlapping agendas and action items	Humility—attribute the best motive to others in their actions and words Faith—confidence that what others say is valuable for me to hear Self-denial—surrender ourselves to the possibility of changing/expanding our perspectives Charity—exercise generosity, fairness, affection

Adapted from Nash, R.J. (2010, May-June). What is the best way to be a social justice advocate? Communication strategies for effective social justice advocacy. *About Campus, 15,* 11–18.

Active Learning Module 11d

Identifying Critical Issues:
Finding Your Passion

Josh Hiscock

> Summary of Concepts

This module addresses Chapter 11, Strategies for Change. In this section, students explore the process of identifying social issues and evaluating what change process they are most passionate about engaging in within the community. The examination of critical issues may be overwhelming for a student. With so many areas needing attention within organizations, institutions, communities, nations, and the world, students face a daunting task of determining where to begin. Finding direction provides focus and a sense of purpose.

Tackling large-scale change as an individual can lead to feelings of hopelessness. For some students, these feelings lead to paralysis that prevents change. Deciding what area to focus on when making a difference may provide the empowerment, motivation, and direction needed to achieve success.

> Learning Outcomes

Students will

- Be able to evaluate a variety of social issues to determine which ones are most salient in their lives.
- Understand the process of making change happen
- Consider the value of partnering with others in the change process
- Apply the components of the Social Change Model of Leadership Development to the process of finding a social issue that stirs passion and interest

> Module Overview

Students view a video about searching for a passion. This highlights the process of defining personal change goals. After an individual reflection exercise, students have the opportunity to share their interests with the full group through a structured activity.

Estimated Time
Activity 1: Passions Video, 20 minutes
Activity 2: Narrowing My Passions, 15 minutes
Activity 3: Headlines, 10-minute activity, 15-minute reflective
  discussion

Materials/Supplies
Video: TED Talk (www.ted.com) titled, "Benjamin Zander: The
  transformative power of classical music"
8-1/2" x 11" paper
Markers
Board or flip charts to write down points emerging from
  discussion

> Module Activities

Activity 1: Passions Video

Time: 20 minutes

Show students the TED talk from Benjamin Zander focused on classical music and passion and how it relates to taking on new possibilities, new experiences, and new connections. This is a good way to segue conversation into asking students what things make them feel passion and a desire to take on new experiences

Video: TED Talk (www.ted.com) titled, "Benjamin Zander: The transformative power of classical music"

Activity 2: Narrowing My Passions

Time: 15 minutes

Students will work independently on this activity. Students will take 10 minutes to answer the following set of questions aimed to aid in the more advanced definition of one's passions. These questions can be placed on a sheet of flip chart paper or distributed on a worksheet.

- About what issues am I the most passionate? Which do I care about the most?
- Who is affected by the issue?
- Am I willing to take the time and make the sacrifices to work on this issue?
- Am I willing to face the challenges associated with this issue?

The instructor should circulate around the room to assist students needing extra guidance. Alternatively, instructors can allow students to work on this activity in groups of two or three.

After 10 minutes, students should begin to address a second set of questions:

- Who are the shareholders or stakeholders who might join me in working with this issue?
- Who is in a position to exert influence—positively or negatively—on the issue?
- Who else might be interested in this project? What other individuals or organizations might I contact?
- How can core participants once identified, be motivated to join the collective effort?
- What do I want to accomplish? Be able to state clearly and succinctly what you are trying to do. Try explaining this to someone who knows nothing about the particular topic or area. This will force you to state things in simple terms that are easy to understand.
- Where can I begin? What person or office should I contact first? The key thing is to begin—starting any project may be frustrating at first.

Activity 3: Headlines

Time: 10 minutes

After students have brainstormed about the issue areas that they find most salient in their lives, instruct them to take a piece of 8-1/2 x 11 inch paper and a marker. Each student should write a single statement on the paper in the form of a newspaper headline that relates to what they wish to accomplish in tacking their passion.

Instruct students to think of recent newspaper headlines as examples. Encourage students to think of this as the one-sentence news bullet that they would want to see printed as the headline of *The New York Times* or *The Washington Post* when their change process is completed. For example, a headline might read "College Graduate Cures Cancer with Help of Professor."

Students should neither place their names on this paper nor use their name in their headline. This portion of the activity should take five minutes.

When completed, students should form a circle with each individual standing shoulder-to shoulder with a neighbor. All participants should place their headline face-down in the middle of the circle. All at once, students should enter the circle to choose a random headline from the pile on the floor, returning to their place in the circle when done. One by one, students should go around the circle and read the headline they selected. For fun, you might ask the group to guess who wrote the head-line. This helps students match passions to people. Go around the entire circle until everyone has had the opportunity to read a headline. This portion of the activity should take 10 minutes.

Debrief, 15 minutes   Following this activity, ask students to return to their seats. If possible, ask students to simply sit down and maintain the circle they created. Begin the activity debrief by using one or more of the following questions:

- What things were salient to you from the activity we just completed?
- What were some of the headlines that you saw that really stood out to you? What about the headline really caught your interest?
- Was there anything that happened during this activity that surprised you?
- How do you see others assisting you in achieving the goal you wrote about in your headline?
- What will your first step be when you leave this workshop to begin to achieve the goal you wrote about in your headline?

> Facilitator Notes

The idea of evaluating social issues and defining one's passions is not easily fit into a 60-minute session. Facilitators may need to be flexible in offering more time in activity two. Activity 1, while a good example of empowering students to action, may be cut from the session to allow more time for self-exploration.

Josh Hiscock is the senior director of alumni benefits and services at The George Washington University. A leadership educator of high school and college students since 2003, Josh's research and professional work focuses on empowering social change and socially responsible leadership.

Learning Module 11e

Appreciative Inquiry

Julie Owen

> Summary of Concepts

This module addresses Chapter 11. This section reviews the concept of Appreciate Inquiry (AI) as a strategy for change. Appreciative Inquiry is a participative process whereby organizational members work to identify what is right in an organization and to leverage these positive, life-giving forces to create provocative propositions for innovation and change. The chapter describes four stages of the inquiry process:

- Discovering periods of excellence and achievement
- Dreaming an ideal organization or community
- Designing new structures and processes
- Delivering the dream

> Learning Outcomes

Students will

- Discover the power of perspective taking and its contribution to eliciting positive moments
- Practice positive inquiry interviews in order to surface life-giving forces
- Experience the power of stories to create shared images of a desired future, in that words create worlds

> Module Overview

Students first learn how to shift their perspectives by examining a space from the vantage points of different professions in order to prepare them for adopting an appreciative lens. Students then practice appreciative interviewing skills in order to experience the life-giving forces or positive core of the Appreciative Inquiry process. Finally, students work to thematize stories and develop provocative propositions of how to innovate a desired future.

Estimated Time

Activity 1: Words Create Worlds, 10-minute small group activity and discussion

Activity 2: The Power of Stories, 30-minute activity, 10-minute reflective discussion

Activity 3: Provocative Propositions, 20-minute individual work and creative sharing

Materials/Supplies

Index cards

Appreciative Interview Guide

Markers

Flip chart paper

Small round stickers to be used for "voting"

Miscellaneous craft materials (pipe cleaners, glue, glitter, construction paper, and so on)

> Module Activities

Activity 1: Words Create Worlds: Developing an Appreciative Focus

Time: 10 minutes

Break students into small groups and give each group an index card with the name of a profession written on it: child care provider, event planner, burglar, fire marshal, custodian, emergency shelter provider, wedding planner, and so forth. Ask groups not to share their assigned professions with each other.

Give the small groups five minutes to explore the room, taking note of what they notice from the perspective of their assigned profession. For example, what assets are present in the room that would benefit the activities of people in such a profession (a window for a burglar to break to enter the room)? In what ways do elements in the room present problems (electric outlets the child care planner will need to cover)?

Ask each small group to share their observations with the full group without naming the profession that was assigned to them. Have the other small groups try to guess the profession by the way the room is described.

Briefly discuss this activity by asking for reflections on the following:

- How did adopting a particular profession or role shape what you noticed or perceived in the room?
- Aside from professions, what other roles, identities, or perspectives shape how we perceive the world?
- How does perception affect interpretation and action?
- How might choosing to adopt a positive or appreciative lens change how a person views a situation?

Activity 2: The Power of Stories and Life-Giving Forces

Time: 30-minute activity, 10-minute reflective discussion

Have students select a partner and conduct a 15-minute interview using the Appreciative Interview Guide provided. Feel free to adapt this template for your specific purposes and circumstances. While the interviewee is answering the questions, the interviewer should record notes about themes and stories discussed and any significant quotes. After 15 minutes have elapsed, have the partners switch roles.

Appreciative Interview Guide/Template (AI interview template is adapted from www.CenterforAppreciativeInquiry.net)

1. *Best Experience*. Tell me a story about the best time you have had with your organization (or team, family, class, community, or other group). Reflecting on your entire experience with that group, recall a time when you felt most alive or excited about your involvement. Describe the event in detail. Over what period of time did it take place? How did it happen? Who else was involved? What made it an exciting or transformative experience?

2. *Values*. Let's discuss some things that you value deeply. Specifically, the things you value about yourself, your work, and your organization.

   - Without being humble, what do you most value about yourself (as a person, as a member of your group or organization, as a friend, and so on)?
   - When you are feeling your best about your work (school work, group work, and so forth), what about the task itself do you value?
   - What is it about your organization (class, team, family, group, community) that you value? What is the single most important thing this group has contributed to your life (or to your learning)?

3. *Life-Giving Forces.* What do you experience as the core value of your organization (class, team, family, group, community)? Give some examples of how you experience these values. What would you like this core value to be? How will you help the group develop this core value?

4. *Three Wishes.* If you had three wishes for this organization, what would they be?

As a large group, discuss the interview process, asking

- Do you find the appreciative approaches come naturally to you? Why or why not?
- What was the most "life-giving" moment of the interview for you as a listener?
- Did any particularly creative or innovative examples emerge from the interview?
- How did sharing positive stories and aspirations for success affect your energy for change?
- What excites or worries you about adopting more asset-based approaches to yourself and your work?

Activity 3: Provocative Propositions: Dreaming an Innovative Future

Time: 20 minutes

Each interviewer should now write two to three themes or life-giving forces they heard in their appreciative interview on a shared piece of flip chart paper. Give each participant three stickers to place next to the themes or ideas that most excite them personally.

Work as a large group to come to a consensus about the theme (with or without supporting subthemes) that they would like to enact in their organization (class, group, community, and so on). Be sure the theme is provocative (stretches or challenges); emerges from a real story or example so that it is possible; and is stated in bold and affirmative terms (Cooperrider, Whitney, & Stavros, 2003).

Have the group quickly and collaboratively create a visual image or metaphor to capture the essence of their chosen theme. Participants may use crafting supplies if they so desire.

Discuss the process of working in both linguistic and artistic ways to capture the essence of group's dream or plan for innovation. Invite group members to make commitments, offers, or requests about how they will help enact this shared vision for change.

> Facilitator Notes

Occasionally you will encounter a student who is resistant to adopting an appreciative approach. Encourage them to experiment with this lens for the duration of the lesson and then to compare it to their preferred way of knowing. You might also model ways to reframe negative responses to appreciative questions. (For example, "Aside from your important critiques, can you think of a time when things did go well?")

The following video clips may be useful to help frame this approach:

An interview with David Cooperrider, the founder of Appreciative Inquiry, available on YouTube, titled "Appreciative Inquiry A Conversation with David Cooperrider."

Dewitt Jones "Celebrating What is Right With the World." Jones is a photographer for *National Geographic* who uses photography as a metaphor for appreciative ways of seeing the world. This video clip is available on YouTube, titled "Dewitt Jones: Finding the Right Answer."

> Reference

Cooperrider, D. L., Whitney, D., & Stavros, J. M. (2003). *Appreciative inquiry handbook: The first in a series of AI workbooks for leaders of change.* Bedford Heights, OH: Lakeshore Communications.

Julie Owen is an assistant professor of leadership and integrative studies at New Century College, George Mason University, where she teaches courses on socially responsible leadership, civic engagement, and community-based research. She is a research scholar for the National Clearinghouse for Leadership Programs and is coeditor of the *Handbook for Student Leadership Development.*

Active Learning Module 12a

Well-Being

Stacey Guenther

> ## Summary of Concepts

This portion of Chapter 12, Thriving Together, introduces four models from positive psychology:

- Tipping Point (Fredrickson, 2007)
- Positive Leadership (Cameron, 2012)
- Domains of Leadership Strengths (Rath & Conchie, 2008)
- PERMA (Seligman, 2011)

The Relational Leadership Model focuses on a leader's ability to cultivate positive relationships. These four models from positive psychology provide background and application for developing positive relationships and for widening the view of what it means, as a leader, to create a positive, productive, engaging environment. For students to glean understanding of what it means to engage as a positive leader focused on a flourishing environment, they must first build self-awareness around their own well-being and positivity.

> Learning Outcomes

Students will

- Consider how well-being and positivity lead to productive, happy environments
- Be able to assess their own levels of well-being

> Module Overview

Students complete and discuss a worksheet to explore their own levels of well-being. Then they engage in an interactive activity related to interpersonal positivity. Finally students are invited to continue their exploration of positivity with a personal experiment.

Estimated Time

Activity 1: Well-Being Worksheet and Discussion
- Individual completion of worksheet: 5 minutes
- Pair sharing of worksheet: 10 minutes
- Small group discussion: 10 minutes
- Large group report out: 10 minutes

Activity 2: Interpersonal Positivity Activity
- Activity: 15 minutes
- Large Group Discussion: 5 minutes

Introduce Positivity Personal Experiment Homework:
5 minutes

Materials/Supplies

Well-Being Worksheets (found in workbook)
Board or flip charts and markers to write down major points emerging from the discussion

❯ Module Activities

Activity 1: Well-Being Worksheet and Discussions

Time: 35 minutes

Have students individually complete the Well-Being Worksheet. In pairs, students then share their completed worksheets, focusing on the following questions:

- What did you notice?
- Were you surprised by the results?
- In what dimensions can you improve your well-being?
- What would it look like if you increased your well-being?

Combine pairs to form small groups and have students brainstorm ideas for increasing well-being. Ask each small group to report their ideas to the whole group.

Variation   Instead of breaking into pairs to share Well-Being Worksheets, you may want to keep the group together to have a large-group discussion using the questions above. Depending upon your group, this may be a powerful time of meaning making.

Activity 2: Interpersonal Positivity Activity

Time: 20 minutes

Adapted from Kat Koppett (2001, pp. 33–37), *Training to Imagine* and the Center for Creative Emergence (www.creativeemergence.com/).

Ask for 10 volunteers. Have them sit or stand in a circle in front of the room while the rest of the group watches, fishbowl-style. Invite the whole group to come up with a fictitious scenario for the volunteers in which they would plan something together; for example, "you're going to create a fund-raising event for the university," or "let's recruit and train a flash mob for the next pep rally."

Each student in the volunteer circle will sequentially, one-by-one, add ideas for the fictitious scenario. The first person will state his or her idea. The next student, and each subsequent student, will begin by responding to the first student's idea with, "Yes, but . . .", and then add their own idea. The circle should continue for 5 minutes.

Ask for a second set of 10 volunteers. Get a second fictitious scenario for this group of volunteers to work with. The instructions will be the same except for one very important difference: instead of starting with "Yes, but . . .", volunteers with begin with, "Yes, and . . ."

The circle should continue for five minutes.

Recruit a third set of 10 volunteers. Ask for a third fictitious scenario. The instructions, once again, will largely be the same. This time, however, students will begin with, "Yes, because . . ." in order to justify the previous student's idea and then continue with "And . . ." by adding their own idea. The circle should continue for 5 minutes.

Facilitate a large-group discussion:

- What did you notice about the three groups?
- What was the "mood" or "energy" of the three different groups?
- How were their ideas different?
- Where did you see positivity emerging?
- How did positivity affect the group's idea generation?
- Based on what you've seen, how might a leader's positivity affect a group?

Variation   If you are working with a team whose purpose is to work together toward a goal, consider using a real, "live" project or event on which the group is actually working in lieu of a factitious scenario.

Positivity Personal Experiment

Invite students to engage in a personal experiment to raise their own well-being and positivity. The experiment should run two (or more) weeks. During the course of the two weeks, students should

1. Write a one- to two-page reflection on how satisfied they feel with life.
2. Daily, practice On Loving Kindness meditation. In her toolkit for increasing positivity and decreasing negativity, Barbara Fredrickson (2009, p. 209) recommends a practice of Loving Kindness, because it targets emotions. Resources for Loving Kindness meditation include:
   - Fredrickson (2009) provides background and a script in her book, *Positivity*.
   - Rick Hanson, best-selling author of *Buddha's Brain: the Practical Neuroscience of Happiness, Love, & Wisdom*, neuropsychologist, and meditation teacher, offers a script found online at his site, www.rickhanson.net.
   - In her book, *Real Happiness: The Power of Meditation,*, Sharon Salzberg (2011) devotes an entire chapter to the Loving Kindness meditation.
   - A guided Loving Kindness meditation featuring Jon Kabat-Zinn, originator of Mindfulness-Based Stress Reduction is available on YouTube, titled, "Heartscape (Loving kindness) {Guided Meditation}."
   - Tara Brach, psychologist and author of *Radical Acceptance*, offers free podcast lectures and guided meditations on her website, www.tarabrach.com. One hour-long talk discusses integrated Loving Kindness meditation, "Divine Abodes: Lovingkindness—October 5, 2011."

3. Daily, complete Barbara Fredrickson's Positivity Ratio tool, found online at www.positivityratio.com. Students will be able to save their results and compare them over time.

4. At least daily, students should do something nice for someone, such as a random act of kindness or something nice for someone close to them, keeping a journal listing these acts. One day each week, students should increase the frequency of these acts to five in one day. Sonja Lyubomirsky (2008, p. 127) found that increasing the intensity in one day can result in significant increases in happiness.

5. Twice per week, students should list at least three things they are grateful for. Resources about gratitude journaling are available through the Greater Good Science Center's website at http://greatergood.berkeley.edu/article/item/tips_for_keeping_a_gratitude_journal.

6. At the end of the two weeks, students should review their positivity ratios, and once again write a one- to two-page reflection on life satisfaction.

7. Recommend students go back and read their first reflection, noting any changes.

Variation   The personal experiment can be altered, substituting different practices in and out. Both Lyubomirsky's (2008) *The How of Happiness* and Fredrickson's (2009) *Positivity* are flush with good ideas for creating a practice to increase joy, positivity, and optimism.

> Facilitator Notes

For more information on the Interpersonal Positivity Activity, refer to *Training to Imagine* by Kat Koppett (2001, pp. 33–41). It may be helpful to ask for volunteers who have had some improvisation experience to include in the group.

> References

Cameron, K. (2012). *Positive leadership: strategies for extraordinary performance*. San Francisco, CA: Berrett-Koehler.

Fredrickson, B. (2009). *Positivity*. New York: Random House.

Koppett, K. (2001). *Training to imagine: Practical improvisational theatre techniques for trainers and managers to enhance creativity, teamwork, leadership and learning*. Sterling, VA: Stylus.

Lyubomirsky, S. (2008). *The how of happiness: A scientific approach to getting the life you want*. New York: Penguin Press.

Rath, T., & Conchie, B. (2008). *Strengths-based leadership: Great leaders, teams, and why people follow*. New York, NY: Gallup Press.

Salzburg, S. (2011). *Real happiness: The power of meditation*. New York, NY: Workman Publishing.

Seligman, M.E.P. (2011). *Flourish: A visionary new understanding of happiness and well-being*. New York, NY: Free Press.

Stacey Guenther is the director of educational programs at the Center for Consciousness and Transformation at George Mason University, where she also earned her master's degree in organization development and knowledge management.

Active Learning Module 12b

⌄
Renewal

Stacey Guenther

◇

> Summary of Concepts

This portion of Chapter 12, Thriving Together, introduces the concept of self-renewal for both leadership development and development of the spirit:

- Stress, unbalance, exhaustion, and overwhelm are likely to detract from leader effectiveness
- Leaders tend to care for others before selves
- Personal renewal as a proactive strategy
- Leaders setting aside time for renewal
- A list of activities for self-renewal includes
  - Try new things
  - Realize what you do matters
  - Keep a personal balance
  - Make time for reflection and centering
  - Maintain positive relationships
  - Prioritize tasks
- Spiritual renewal involves leading from values, meaning and purpose, and being connected to the world

> Learning Outcomes

Students will

* Learn about the concept of self-renewal and how it may apply to them
* Explore ways of generating their own self-renewal

> Module Overview

Lead students through an exploration of renewal practices so they may consider what is most important for their individual experience and find what practices they most enjoy. The final activity, a brainstorm of on-campus resources, will extend the exploration.

Facilitate a large-group discussion about renewal and balance, why it is important, and what happens when they don't have self-care and balance in their lives.

Estimated Time

Activity 1: Reflecting on Renewal and Balance
* Reflective writing: 5 minutes
* Small group sharing: 10 minutes
* Report out: 5 minutes

Activity 2: Breathing Break
* Breathing practice: 5 minutes
* Discussion: 5 minutes

Activity 3: Savoring the Good
* Savoring practice: 5 minutes
* Discussion: 5 minutes

Activity 4: Resource Brainstorm
* Small Group Discussions: 5 minutes
* Report Out: 10 minutes

Homework: Creating a Spiritual Development Plan (5 minutes)

Materials/Supplies
Board or flip charts and markers to write down major points
emerging from the discussion

> Module Activities

Activity 1: Reflect on Renewal and Balance

Time: 20 minutes

- Students will write reflectively on how life balance. They can
  consider
  - Basic self-care—how well are they eating? How much sleep
    do they get? Do they exercise or engage in physical activity
    on a regular basis?
  - How much of their time do they spend doing things that
    "fill their tanks"—things they really enjoy and get a posi-
    tive charge from?
  - How much stress do they have in their lives, and what do
    they do to manage the stress?
- In small groups, discuss what they've just written about. What
  are common threads that emerge?
- Small groups report out to large group.

Activity 2: Breathing Break

Time: 10 minutes

In *Real Happiness*, Sharon Salzberg says taking a "mini-
meditation" is "grabbing a centering moment . . . to connect
with a deeper sense of yourself." She goes on to say that these
breathing breaks help us to restore calm and to connect with
what really matters (p. 56).

- Tell students you will be engaging in a brief centering exercise.
- Dim lights.

- Instruct students to sit with both feet on the floor, backs straight in the their chairs, eyes closed or gazing downward, and in silence.
- Instruct students to focus on their breathing, just paying attention to the in-breath and out-breath but not controlling, changing, or altering.
- Notice the sensation of the cold air on their noses as they breathe.
- Notice their chest or bellies rising and falling as they breathe in and out.
- During the activity, instruct students that if they notice their minds wandering to gently redirect their attention back on their breathing.
- Continue the breathing break for four to five minutes.
- At the end, ask students what the experience was like for them and how they are feeling.

Activity 3: Savoring the Good

Time: 10 minutes

Taken from *One Good Thing: Developing a Buddha Brain One Simple Practice at a Time* by Rick Hanson (2011, pp. 19–21).

1. Think of something good that has happened in the past 12, 24, 36 hours. It doesn't have to be something big, but it can be.
2. Take in the experience and focus on the positive aspects of it, as well as the positive emotions connected to it.
3. Hold yourself there for 30 seconds and imagine the feel-good experience soaking into your body.

By savoring positive experiences, Hanson says that the positive balances the negative and helps "put the challenges in perspective, lift your energy and spirits, highlight useful resources, and fill up your own cup so you have more to offer to others" (p. 19). Hanson recommends engaging in this practice as often as possible, even several times a day.

4. Following the practice, ask students how the practice was for them.

Activity 4: Sources of Renewal on Campus

Time: 15 minutes

- In small groups, students will brainstorm places, organizations, and events found on campus that may be sources of renewal for themselves and other students.
- Small groups report out creating a master list.

Homework: Creating a Spiritual Development Plan

Time: 5 minutes

Astin, Astin, and Lindholm (2011, p. 4) define spirituality as having " . . . to do with the values that we hold most dear, our sense of who we are and where we come from, our beliefs about why we are here—the meaning and purpose that we see in our work and our life—and our sense of connectedness to one another and to the world around us." In their book, *Cultivating the Spirit: How College Can Enhance Students' Inner Lives*, the authors measured spiritual development through measures of equanimity, ecumenical worldview, ethic of caring, charitable involvement, and spiritual quest. The authors found that the most beneficial means of students developing spiritually is to engage in the following activities:

- *Service learning*: taking courses that involve engaging with non-profit and community organizations.
- *Volunteer work*: volunteering time for a charity or service organization.
- *Studying abroad*: spending a semester outside of the United States in an academic program for credit.

- *Exploring spiritual traditions*: joining a spiritual community, being part of an organization exploring spirituality, or taking classes that involve reading sacred texts and discussion spiritual traditions.
- *Engaging in contemplative practices*: engaging in a regular practice such as yoga, meditation, tai chi, qigong, prayer, or practices that are similarly contemplative.

Students will create a plan detailing how they will engage with at least three of the areas during their college careers. The purpose of this assignment is for students to create intentions around developing the spirit, which is a source of long-term renewal.

> Facilitator Notes

The main purpose of this module is for students to build awareness around their own self-care and renewal and then to provide some practices for them to experiment with. There are many, many practices that would fit here, so instructors should consider their own experience and resources both within their groups and campuses as appropriate to add. You could consider

- Yoga stretching.
- Mindful movements and/or walking (this would be a good choice on a nice day).
- Referring back to Chapter 4 and those modules to use strengths as a source of renewal.
- Artistic activities. An easy and popular activity is coloring mandalas. Search the Internet for "mandalas to color."

❯ References

Astin, A. W., Astin, H. S., & Lindholm, J. A. (2010). *Cultivating the spirit: How college can enhance students' inner lives.* San Francisco, CA: Jossey-Bass.

Salzburg, S. (2011). *Real happiness: The power of meditation.* New York, NY: Workman Publishing.

Stacey Guenther is the director of educational programs at the Center for Consciousness and Transformation at George Mason University, where she also earned her master's degree in organization development and knowledge management.